A Guide to
Mathematics
Coaching

A Guide to
Mathematics
Coaching

Processes for
Increasing Student
Achievement

Ted H. Hull
Don S. Balka
Ruth Harbin Miles

CORWIN
A SAGE Company

For information:

Corwin
A SAGE Company
2455 Teller Road
Thousand Oaks,
    California 91320
(800) 233-9936
Fax: (800) 417-2466
www.corwinpress.com

SAGE Pvt. Ltd.
B 1/I 1 Mohan Cooperative
    Industrial Area
Mathura Road, New Delhi 110 044
India

SAGE Ltd.
1 Oliver's Yard
55 City Road
London EC1Y 1SP
United Kingdom

SAGE Asia-Pacific Pte. Ltd.
33 Pekin Street #02-01
Far East Square
Singapore 048763

Printed in the United States of America.

Library of Congress Cataloging-in-Publication Data

Hull, Ted H.
A guide to mathematics coaching: Processes for increasing student achievement/Ted H. Hull, Don Balka, Ruth Harbin Miles.
        p. cm.
Includes bibliographical references and index.
ISBN 978-1-4129-7263-5 (cloth)
ISBN 978-1-4129-7264-2 (pbk.)

    1. Mathematics teachers—Training of. 2. Mathematics—Study and teaching. 3. Personal coaching. 4. Mentoring in education. I. Balka, Don. II. Miles, Ruth Harbin. III. Title.

QA16.H85 2009
510.71—dc22   2009006368

This book is printed on acid-free paper.

09   10   11   12   13   10   9   8   7   6   5   4   3   2   1

Acquisitions Editor:	Cathy Hernandez
Editorial Assistant:	Sarah Bartlett
Production Editor:	Libby Larson
Developmental Editor:	Donovan Walling
Copy Editor:	Cate Huisman
Typesetter:	C&M Digitals (P) Ltd.
Proofreader:	Wendy Jo Dymond
Indexer:	Terri Corry
Cover and Graphic Designer:	Rose Storey

Contents

List of Figures

Preface

Mathematics is the new literacy. Studies show that achievement in mathematics is strongly linked to career opportunities and personal economic success (National Mathematics Advisory Panel, 2008). To ensure bright futures for all students, mathematics learning, understanding, and achievement must increase. Under pressure to improve mathematics achievement, district leaders, campus leaders, and mathematics teachers are vulnerable to grasping at quick fix ideas that may waste financial resources and time. Unfortunately, there is no magic elixir or silver bullet. Increasing mathematics achievement is a rigorous and challenging goal that will take concerted effort and time, yet it can be reached.

Mathematics coaching shows promise as an effective method of changing teacher practice and improving student achievement. Mathematics coaches are positioned to see and impact the daily teaching practice of classroom teachers. Yet they also are positioned to see the much broader picture of what is happening schoolwide and at the district level. They are able to view the content organization and delivery both horizontally and vertically. They are positioned to be an important component in improving student learning. However, the roles, responsibilities, and duties of mathematics coaches are not always clear to coaches and the teachers who work with them.

If mathematics coaches turn to current research to better understand their roles and to determine a direction for their work, they will be disappointed. The research that is available focuses primarily upon either principals and effective leadership strategies or generalized content coaching recommendations. The guidance and suggestions offered are not specific to mathematics, nor are they presented as part of a developmental process that has been thoughtfully designed.

Confusion about their roles and the lack of a developmental process are key challenges faced by mathematics coaches. These challenges are exacerbated if school leaders have launched a coaching initiative with little preparation or planning for success through supportive internal structures. Coaches, formerly strong and effective classroom teachers, occupy a unique place in the education system, a place that is sometimes defined by what they are not. Coaches are not classroom teachers, supervisors, coordinators, or administrators. Even more, they may not actually "belong" to any particular school, nor do they "belong" to a central office. In all likelihood, messages about what they are not have already been made vividly clear to coaches in both obvious and subtle ways. What has failed to be communicated is who mathematics coaches *are* and what they can do. Instead, many coaches have been left to their own devices to figure out their job—where to work, who to work with, what to do, and how to actually increase student learning.

Effective coaching requires a range of skills, strategies, techniques, and practices. It is much more than any one method, such as conducting demonstration lessons for classroom teachers to emulate behind closed doors. Coaches tackle the necessary work of removing the walls that isolate teachers and initiating processes of productive collaboration. The good news is that professional, adult contact is valued and appreciated by most teachers. They want and need feedback on their instructional performance if they are to be effective, and they seek to constantly improve. Rather than offering feedback that is primarily evaluative, mathematics coaches offer supportive, nurturing, and practical guidance. Providing this support and information is a job that is tailor-made for coaches. Even so, entering classrooms and working with teachers poses challenges. Coaches may wonder "How can I build trust with my teachers? How do I get them to welcome me into their classrooms? How do I provide meaningful feedback? What is my responsibility in working with reluctant or difficult teachers?"

While countless books on effective leadership have been published in recent years, most of these address leaders in line authority positions, such as principals and superintendents—those with the power to hire or fire, reward or punish, and promote or demote. Other staff members, such as coordinators and supervisors, have lesser decision-making authority. Mathematics coaches hold a unique position as leaders. Their primary responsibility is to work with classroom teachers to increase student learning by implementing decisions made by leaders in line authority positions. Mathematics coaches influence instruction by building trusting relationships, challenging ineffective instructional practices, supporting teachers as they learn new practices, providing meaningful and focused feedback, and implementing manageable, effective improvement processes. As any practicing mathematics coach knows, the role is complex and challenging.

Yet coaches *can* successfully initiate effective mathematics teaching and focus on critical coaching actions that will close the achievement gap and lead to equity. Engaging teachers in the processes of clarifying and aligning the curriculum and planning and teaching effective lessons will help transform mathematics classrooms and ensure equity.

This book was written to offer manageable, practical advice to mathematics content coaches in order to clarify, define, and fulfill their very important role. The primary audiences for this book are mathematics coaches; those who work with or supervise mathematics coaches, such as principals and central office personnel; and those making districtwide or school decisions about mathematics coaching. A developmental, sequential process for engaging in the work of mathematics coaching is presented. The process provides coaches with a leverage point—a place from which to begin the work with teachers and have an immediate impact on student achievement, thereby providing opportunities for more effective coaching contact in the future. The information presented here is intended to help clarify expectations and to increase the likelihood that mathematics coaching will have the desired impact on student learning.

Each chapter builds on the guidance and recommendations of the previous chapter toward a high-quality mathematics program. This process incorporates the National Council of Teachers of Mathematics' principles of equity, curriculum, teaching, learning, and assessment as described in *Principles and Standards for School Mathematics* (2000) as well as the leadership principles advocated by the National Council of Supervisors of Mathematics and published in *The PRIME Leadership Framework: Principles and Indicators for Mathematics Education Leaders* (2008).

The knowledge, skills, and complementing actions that are addressed throughout the chapters of the book are separated into three parts:

I.   Preparing the Foundation

   Chapter 1: Defining Mathematics Coaching

   Chapter 2: Bridging From the Present to the Future

   Chapter 3: Building Rapport With Teachers

II. Mathematics Coaching Model

   Chapter 4: Focusing on the Curriculum

   Chapter 5: Implementing the Curriculum as Designed

   Chapter 6: Planning and Coteaching Lessons

CHAPTER DESCRIPTIONS

Chapter 1 defines a *mathematics coach* as an individual who is well versed in mathematics content and pedagogy and who works directly with classroom teachers to improve student learning of mathematics. In order to fulfill this role, mathematics coaches need to possess certain characteristics, including knowledge of adult learning styles and strategies, group dynamics, and social norms. They must understand data acquisition, analysis, interpretation, and application. And they need to know about confidentiality and trust-building.

In Chapter 2, "Bridging From the Present to the Future," we show coaches how to assess the current state of schools and classrooms on an improvement continuum, and we offer a framework for the development of a high-quality mathematics program.

The content of Chapter 3, "Building Rapport With Teachers," provides practical advice to help coaches establish and build trust and rapport with classroom teachers. Coaching scenarios demonstrate how coaches can respond effectively in a variety of situations. Examples are drawn from real-life situations that coaches are likely to encounter.

Chapter 4, "Focusing on the Curriculum," provides a process by which coaches may initiate working with teachers in a nonthreatening way that directly and positively impacts student learning and achievement. Ensuring that all students have the opportunity to learn is an important part of the work of coaches and a critical point in moving toward equity.

In Chapter 5, "Implementing the Curriculum as Designed," coaches are shown how to gather data about the extent to which teachers are implementing the mathematics curriculum and how to provide feedback to classroom teachers. An aligned curriculum forms a solid foundation and leads to the next step in the process, planning and coteaching lessons.

Chapter 6, "Planning and Coteaching Lessons," focuses on the implementation of effective classroom instructional strategies to increase student learning. By helping teachers plan effective lessons, coaches are able both to assess what teachers are currently able to do and to encourage adjustment in lessons, so instruction is more research based and provides for active student participation. As lesson planning with teachers continues, it becomes quite natural for coaches to become coteachers for selected lessons. This joint planning reduces the stress levels and purposely moves coaches into classrooms.

Chapter 7, "Making Student Thinking Visible," provides strategies for helping teachers move from a traditional, less effective model of mathematics instruction to an alternative method of instruction that incorporates high-effect, research-based instructional strategies and helps teachers better understand student thinking and respond accordingly.

"Analyzing and Reflecting on Lessons," discussed in Chapter 8, follows from collaborative planning and coteaching. Coaches initiate a lesson analysis process by discussing their part of the lesson, thereby modeling the process of reflecting upon student actions and evidence of student learning.

By this stage of the process, coaches will have established professional working relationships and a high degree of trust and rapport with teachers. This degree of rapport and trust lays the groundwork for "Charting Long-Term Progress," discussed in Chapter 9. Coaches, in order to stay focused on critical elements of change, draw upon trend data. Teachers are developing a true sense of efficacy and can see a relationship between their actions in the classroom and student learning. Teachers also are better able to consider areas for improvement. This connection and sense of efficacy are vitally important to sustaining change initiatives, and they complete the Mathematics Coaching Model.

In Chapter 10, "Working Within the Education System," we examine how mathematics coaches build collegial partners and groups for planning, analyzing, and reflecting, actively assisting teachers and leaders in establishing both formal and informal networks.

The book ends with Chapter 11, where coaches are given strategies and encouragement to continue "Sustaining Momentum" for change. This chapter examines processes that support adult change and institutional change. We discuss the reality of fluctuations in change: spurts of improvement followed by brief periods of stagnation or even decline. We encourage coaches to focus on the bigger picture of trend changes rather than daily fluctuations of individual behaviors.

The end of the book is actually a beginning, since the process described is highly recursive. We encourage coaches to repeat the process, cycling through the activities and recommendations, at increasingly higher levels of performance. We challenge coaches to critically analyze where they are in terms of communication and understanding about their job, to think about the rapport they have established and where more attention is needed, and to use trend data to determine which areas of the mathematics curriculum are still misaligned. Coaches may do the same for planning, teaching, and analyzing. The improvement cycle does not end, but spirals upward.

The recommendations and actions contained within this book reside within the control of mathematics coaches and may, therefore, be immediately implemented. Through their positive, supportive actions, mathematics coaches can bring hope and encouragement to classroom teachers and play a critical role in advancing mathematics achievement for all students.

Acknowledgments

Corwin gratefully acknowledges the contributions of the following reviewers:

Cheryl Avalos, Mathematics Consultant
Hacienda Heights, CA

Joyce Fischer, Assistant Professor of Mathematics
Texas State University
San Marcos, TX

Diane Kinch, Secondary Mathematics Specialist
Pomona Unified School District
Pomona, CA

Renée Peoples, K–5 Mathematics Coach
Swain County Schools
Bryson City, NC

Gail Underwood, Mathematics Coach
Grant Elementary School & Field Elementary School
Columbia, MO

Lois Williams, Regional Faculty
Mary Baldwin College
Staunton, VA

About the Authors

Ted H. Hull completed 32 years of service in public education before retiring and opening Hull Educational Consulting. He served as a mathematics teacher, K–12 mathematics coordinator, middle school principal, and director of curriculum and instruction as well as project director for the Charles A. Dana Center at the University of Texas in Austin. While at the University of Texas (2001–2005) he directed the research project Transforming Schools: Moving From Low-Achieving to High-Performing Learning Communities. As part of the project, Ted worked directly with district leaders, school administrators, and teachers in Arkansas, Oklahoma, Louisiana, and Texas to develop instructional leadership skills and implement effective mathematics instruction.

Ted is a regular presenter at local, state, and national meetings. He has written numerous articles for the newsletter of the National Council of Supervisors of Mathematics (NCSM), including "Understanding the Six Steps of Implementation: Engagement by an Internal or External Facilitator" (2005) and "Leadership Equity: Moving Professional Development Into the Classroom" (2005) as well as "Manager to Instructional Leader" (2007) for the *NCSM Journal of Mathematics Education Leadership.* He published "Teacher Input Into Classroom Visits: Customized Classroom Visit Form" in the *Texas Mathematics Teacher* (2006). Ted was also a contributing author for publications from the Charles A. Dana Center: *Mathematics Standards in the Classroom: Resources for Grades 6–8* (2002) and *Middle School Mathematics Assessments: Proportional Reasoning* (2004). He is an active member of the Texas Association of Supervisors of Mathematics and served on the NCSM board of directors as regional director for Southern 2. Ted lives with his wife, Susan, in Pflugerville, Texas.

Don S. Balka, a former middle school and high school mathematics teacher, is professor emeritus in the mathematics department at Saint Mary's College, Notre Dame, Indiana. During his career as an educator, Don has presented over 2,000 workshops on the use of manipulatives with elementary and secondary students at national and regional conferences of the National Council of Teachers of Mathematics (NCTM), state mathematics conferences, and inservice training sessions for school districts throughout the United States. In addition, he has taught classes in schools throughout the world, including Ireland, Scotland, England, Saudi Arabia, Italy, Greece, Japan, and the Mariana Islands in the South Pacific. Don has written over 20 books on the use of manipulatives for teaching K–12 mathematics and is a coauthor of the Macmillan K–5 elementary mathematics series, *Math Connects.* He has served on the boards of directors of the NCTM, NCSM, and the School Science and Mathematics Association. Don resides with his wife, Sharon, in LaPaz, Indiana.

Ruth Harbin Miles coaches rural, suburban, and inner-city school mathematics teachers. Her professional experience includes coordinating the K–12 mathematics teaching and learning program for the Olathe, Kansas, public schools for over 25 years; teaching mathematics methods courses at Virginia's Mary Baldwin College and at Ottawa, Mid America Nazarene, St. Mary's, and Fort Hays state universities in Kansas; and serving as president of the Kansas Association of Teachers of Mathematics. She represented eight midwestern states on the board of directors for NCSM and has been a copresenter for NCSM's leadership professional development national conferences. Ruth is the coauthor of *Walkway to the Future: How to Implement the NCTM Standards* (Jansen Publications, 1996) and is one of the writers for NCSM's *PRIME Leadership Framework* (2008). As co-owner of Happy Mountain Learning, she specializes in developing teachers' content knowledge and strategies for engaging students to meet high standards of achievement in mathematics. Ruth resides with her husband, Samuel, near the Blue Ridge Mountains in Madison, Virginia.

Part I

Preparing the Foundation

1 Defining Mathematics Coaching

Does coaching work? Can mathematics coaches make a difference? These are real questions in an ongoing debate about the value of content coaching. According to the National Mathematics Advisory Panel (2008), research that supports coaching is sparse and inconclusive, but so is research refuting it. We believe that the key question should not be whether coaching works but under what conditions. The answer to this question is supported by several beliefs:

- Professionals in many fields rely on coaches to help them perfect their skills (Knight, 2007; West & Staub, 2003).
- Teacher isolation is a deterrent to improving professional skills (Short & Greer, 2002; Williams, 1996).
- Professional development that is specifically related to classroom instruction and student learning is effective (Loucks-Horsley, Love, Stiles, Mundry, & Hewson, 2003; York-Barr, Sommers, Ghere, & Montie, 2001).
- Opportunities to learn appropriate content and curriculum alignment help teachers close the achievement gap (Adelman, 2006; Conzemius & O'Neill, 2001; English, 2000; Marzano, 2003).
- Students can achieve when they have access to high-quality teaching and effective programs (Loucks-Horsley et al., 2003; National Council of Teachers of Mathematics, 2000; National Research Council, 2004b).
- Student learning is increased when high-quality programs are adopted, implemented, supported, and sustained (National Research Council, 2004b).

All of these beliefs point the way to what coaches can do to help teachers teach most effectively.

WHAT IS A MATHEMATICS COACH?

The term *coach* is part of our everyday vocabulary, but what do educators mean when they use it? Most people think of sports coaches first and then realize that there are many kinds of coaches. Music coaches train individuals to play various musical instruments. Voice coaches work with singers, public speakers, and vocal performers. Acting coaches work with actors.

In schools, just as sports coaches work with teams and individual athletes, there are other coaches who work with students to improve their academic skills, for example, for the University Interscholastic League competitions that cross many areas of school life, from writing to business to using calculators. The idea of employing coaches to enhance skills is accepted in our society and our schools (West & Staub, 2003).

But this is the critical point: People form mental images of what a coach is, and these images influence their thoughts and actions. To gain a clear understanding of what a mathematics coach is and does, it is helpful to build a definition in stages:

1. Defining *mathematics coach* for purposes of this book.

2. Identifying the responsibilities of mathematics coaches.

3. Identifying characteristics of successful mathematics coaches.

4. Dispelling negative images.

By working through these stages, readers will be able to develop a mental filter so that they can focus on the critical components of successful mathematics coaching.

STAGE 1: DEFINING *MATHEMATICS COACH*

Simply stated, *a mathematics coach is an individual who is well versed in mathematics content and pedagogy and who works directly with classroom teachers to improve student learning of mathematics.*

This definition describes the knowledge base required for effective mathematics coaching. The coach is

- well versed in mathematics content and
- well versed in pedagogy.

This definition also describes the actual work of effective mathematics coaching. The coach

- engages in direct contact with classroom teachers and
- works to improve student learning.

In a book of essays on coaching, Felux and Snowdy (2006, p. ix) note, "Different titles exist for this position—math coach, math specialist, math support teacher, math resource teacher, and more. And just as there isn't consistency with my colleagues' titles, there isn't much consistency with their responsibilities."

The term *coach* can be elusive and even emotionally charged. It can refer to various responsibilities. So what is the essential aspect? Marilyn Burns offers a starting point: "With all of the variations and differences, a common goal guides math coaches—to support the mathematics learning of all students by supporting teachers to improve their teaching of mathematics" (Felux & Snowdy, 2006, p. ix).

The keywords are *support* and *improve*. A mathematics coach

- supports mathematics learning,
- supports teachers,
- improves students' learning, and
- improves teachers' teaching.

In order to coach teachers successfully, the mathematics coach must be knowledgeable and capable of direct, effective interaction with teachers. Generally coaches are seen as supporting and encouraging. They continually analyze strengths and weaknesses and build on these findings to help teachers improve instruction so that students' learning improves.

To some this may sound similar to the definition of a *mentor*. Thus, it is important to distinguish between a coach and a mentor. They are different roles. We will not use *mentor* and *coach* interchangeably.

A mentor is an experienced staff person who is assigned to work with a colleague new to the school or the profession. For example, a mentor might assist a new teacher in learning about the school's policies and procedures. This definition of *mentor* excludes individuals directly assigned to work with classroom teachers in improving the teaching and learning process, whom we define as coaches.

This is an important distinction, because these two roles often are confused or blended by administrators or policy makers. To be effective as mathematics coaches, individuals in this role need to be able to distinguish what they do from what mentors typically do. The distinction will become clearer as we identify the responsibilities of mathematics coaches.

STAGE 2: IDENTIFYING RESPONSIBILITIES

Mathematics coaches usually are not assigned to teach classes on a daily basis; they work with teachers who are.

To start, coaches view the big picture of mathematics teaching and learning. Then they focus on identifying particular program strengths and weaknesses. Their purpose is to improve the whole by improving individual components of the mathematics program, and they base this work on National Council of Teachers of Mathematics (NCTM) principles. These principles guide but do not provide a road map. Coaches must determine their course of action on their own, often with little support. The job is demanding, and there is no coach to coach them.

Coaches must support—often stimulate—change. Frequently, that is explicitly what they are hired to do. Coaches' responsibilities should be viewed as part of change processes. The first responsibility of improving students' mathematics achievement cannot be accomplished if something is not changed. The age-old expression holds true: If you always do what you have always done, you will always get what you have always gotten.

Mathematics coaches lead change efforts that are manageable, significant, and within the purview of the coaches and that have a positive effect on student learning. Hall and Hord (2001) state, "Change is not only, however, about the implementors—those who will change their practices—but also about those who will facilitate the implementors in doing so" (p. 27). Mathematics coaches are those who "facilitate the implementors."

To this end, the responsibilities of mathematics coaches can be summarized as follows: They

- work with teachers to improve mathematics achievement,
- manage and control curriculum and instructional materials,
- manage and regulate professional development,
- monitor program implementation,
- build the mathematics program by using its strengths and reducing its weaknesses,
- maintain and share best-practice research,
- build collaborative teams and networks, and
- gather, analyze, and interpret data, such as from assessments and benchmark tests, to inform instruction.

These responsibilities are interconnected; each is part of the whole. Even though mathematics coaches may select one of these to concentrate on at a particular time, the power of coaching resides in understanding how these responsibilities interrelate and influence one another.

Just as mathematical knowledge and skills are not effectively taught in isolation, neither can mathematics coaches work on these responsibilities without taking several into consideration. For example, building collaborative teams of teachers is not an end but a beginning. The coaches' jobs are complex and time consuming. Getting one job done can seem like a major accomplishment, but in reality, that job may be only one component that supports an entire spectrum of responsibilities.

Another example might go like this: A mathematics coach intent on raising student achievement necessarily must work on improving curriculum and instruction. This translates into ongoing assessment that leads to pruning ineffective or misaligned parts of the curriculum and replacing them with effective, aligned components. The changed curriculum may require new professional learning, which the coach also must organize and deliver.

STAGE 3: IDENTIFYING CHARACTERISTICS

If mathematics coaches are to perform successfully their various responsibilities, it follows that these individuals need to possess certain characteristics in the form of knowledge and understandings. These characteristics are indicators, not requirements. Individuals naturally differ in the extent of their knowledge, and some characteristics dominate others. Following are basic knowledge components for successful coaches:

> **Mathematics Content.** Coaches should understand the developmental nature of mathematics and the interconnections among concepts. They also need to know and understand the content contained in state and district standards as well as assessment concepts and requirements. They should understand the purposes and rationales undergirding the adoption of instructional materials and their organization and use in teaching.

> **Pedagogy.** Coaches should be familiar with current research on how students learn and understand how to translate research findings into effective instruction, particularly for underachieving students or students with a primary language other than English. They should know what motivates and engages students in learning at various stages of growth and development.

Adult Learning Styles and Strategies. Coaches should understand adult learning and know how to influence adults to cause change in their beliefs and actions. Coaches need to be effective listeners so that they can appropriately use strategies to motivate resistant teachers by building rapport and bringing them into change initiatives.

Group Dynamics and Social Norms. Coaches should know and be able to use consensus-building strategies. Often the successful use of such strategies depends on a coach's ability to clearly communicate in group settings in ways that are respectful and supportive. Coaches need to understand social norms—various ways that people send and receive messages—and to be alert to all methods of communication, such as those described by Kaser and colleagues (2002), including

- body language,
- physical presence,
- ability and willingness to listen,
- accessibility and openness,
- words, and
- behavior. (p. 50)

Coaches should believe in the power of groups, understand synergy (when the whole is greater than the sum of its parts), and strive to build collaborative communities of adult learners.

Data Acquisition, Analysis, Interpretation, and Application. Coaches should understand the power of data. Data are used to chart progress and maintain motivation, to inform instructional practices, and to ensure that students are learning appropriate content. Data must be accurate, relevant, and timely. Thus, effective coaches know how to collect data and then analyze and organize data for interpretation and application.

Confidentiality and Trust-Building. Coaches have spheres of influence. They are charged with improving mathematics teaching and learning, but their responsibilities also overlap with those of others, from teachers to superintendents. They must coordinate their efforts with these individuals and maintain healthy professional relationships, which can be done only if the coaches can be trusted in professional matters.

STAGE 4: DISPELLING NEGATIVE IMAGES

Coach ought to convey a positive connotation, but that is not always the case. If *coach* is seen as negative, it can undermine the best efforts of mathematics coaches.

Peter Senge and his colleagues (2000) propose the idea of mental models, or images, that form the foundations of beliefs and influence actions. They state, "Our behavior and our attitudes are shaped by the images, assumptions, and stories that we carry in our minds of ourselves, other people, institutions, and every aspect of the world" (p. 67). These mental models usually reside below the level of awareness and are rarely tested or examined. This is the issue for mathematics coaches: If a teacher's mental model of a coach is someone who is demanding or temperamental (or if the teacher harbors any other negative association with coaches), then actions taken by the coach, however positive in intent, will be filtered through this negative image. The result will be resistance to the actions.

Coaches must balance their self-images with the mental model of a coach held by the teachers with whom they work. These images need to match as much as possible. For example, a teacher may not believe that a mathematics coach belongs in his or her classroom, because the coach's visits could interfere with instruction, disrupt the lesson, disturb the students, and so forth. This teacher might view a coach's job as managing materials and developing curriculum, perhaps occasionally helping with planning lessons or training. To be effective with this teacher, the coach will need to correct this image, first by identifying the teacher's mental model and then by working with the teacher to create a more positive understanding of the coach's role and responsibilities.

CRITICAL POINTS

In summary, the definition of *mathematics coach* is straightforward:

A mathematics coach is an individual who is well versed in mathematics content and pedagogy and who works directly with classroom teachers to improve student learning of mathematics.

This definition is best understood in terms of supporting teachers and improving both students' and teachers' learning. Mathematics coaches have a variety of responsibilities, all of which lead to the bottom line: change. Coaches are employed to be change agents. In order to fulfill this role, they should possess certain characteristics, including knowledge of adult learning styles and strategies, group dynamics, and social norms. They need to understand data acquisition, analysis, interpretation, and application. And they should know about confidentiality and trust-building. Finally, to be successful, coaches need to be able to correct negative images about what coaching means and what coaches do.

2 Bridging From the Present to the Future

In Chapter 1 we identified characteristics and responsibilities that support a definition of *mathematics coach* as "an individual who is well versed in mathematics content and pedagogy and who works directly with classroom teachers to improve student learning of mathematics." In this chapter we examine some of the specific problems that mathematics coaches may encounter and what they can do to solve them. If certain problems are "the present," then what vision should define "the future" in which those problems are solved?

GOALS, PROCEDURES, AND SHARED VISION

A starting point will be to expand the understanding of the mathematics coach's role and responsibilities. Teachers and administrators with whom the coach will work need to understand what the coach seeks to do and why. Three points are key:

- The definition of *mathematics coach* should be understood by all parties.
- The responsibilities of the coach need to be identified and commonly agreed on.
- The characteristics needed to be a successful coach should be known and addressed.

These understandings cannot be achieved in a single conversation but will be gained through continual contact and communication over time.

And time-consuming though it may be, such communication is an important foundation for change. Lack of clarity on one or more of these points can create confusion and potentially derail a coach's efforts.

Part of understanding the mathematics coach's role and responsibilities will come with knowing what coaching aims to achieve and how the coach will go about creating and instilling change. First, the goal of coaching is to improve mathematics teaching and learning. Two primary indicators will signal success in reaching this goal:

1. Mathematics achievement scores on all measures will increase.

2. Mathematics achievement gaps among subgroups will decrease.

Second, the coaching of teachers is essential to effecting change in mathematics classrooms and achieving this goal.

Improving mathematics teaching and learning through direct coaching of teachers is a complex goal with both primary and secondary effects. The primary effects are the numbered indicators above. But the secondary effects also are important, because they include reinforcement or support for teachers' actions to achieve the main goal. For example, a secondary effect of increasing students' learning is that mathematics teachers feel empowered by a sense of efficacy—a deepened belief that what they do in the classroom directly affects student learning. This sense of efficacy encourages additional classroom changes and new efforts to improve instruction, increases teachers' sense of purpose and mission, and undoubtedly leads some teachers to decide to remain in the profession who might otherwise have chosen a different career path. Success also affects the level of students' engagement, students' willingness to be challenged, and students' confidence in their ability to succeed in higher levels of mathematics (National Research Council [NRC], 2004a). The procedures that drive improvement are many and vary according to conditions in individual schools and classrooms, but they are grounded by a shared vision. This vision should encompass the characteristics of a high-quality mathematics program, which is demonstrated by principles in action. For example, this vision should clarify expectations in order to increase the likelihood that mathematics coaching will have the desired effect. It needs to provide a ruler, or a gauge, against which to measure progress toward the goal and thus to know whether the actions are working.

One approach to creating a clearly defined vision is to examine what is happening in classrooms now—the present—and what should be happening in classrooms in order to reach the goal of improving teaching and learning—the future. This can be thought of as a continuum that extends from the present to the future. Where is the school or classroom on this continuum of mathematics improvement, and where does it want to be? When these questions are answered, then the resulting vision can guide coaches and teachers in selecting procedures that move classroom instruction and student achievement along the continuum toward the desired future.

A shared vision helps to focus the work of coaches and teachers, but coaches are tasked with the leadership role. Coaches have the responsibility of pulling teachers together to build the vision collaboratively; coaches are initiators and resource providers. They start the change action by serving as a catalyst, by introducing teachers to new information about classroom practices supported by research, and by engaging teachers in meaningful professional conversations. Without this foundational work by coaches, working in collaboration with teachers, it will be difficult to achieve meaningful change. Alignment of understandings and expectations seldom happens by accident.

Teachers also can play leadership roles. For example, teacher leaders (and potential future coaches) can be reviewers of research and lead innovators. These teachers are vital to the engagement of others in the collaborative work of envisioning the future toward which all will work.

Before any change process can begin, it is necessary not only to envision the future but also to understand the present. In this aspect, too, leadership responsibility falls to the coaches. For mathematics coaches to address actions and skills necessary for change, they need to know the current status of mathematics teaching and learning in the school or classroom. This is important not only for beginning but also for continuing change processes. If mathematics coaches cannot routinely determine the current status of a classroom in terms of teaching and learning, then they will not be able to determine progress. And if progress is being made and change is occurring, then the status will constantly be changing. Therefore, mathematics coaches need methods for determining a classroom's current status so that they can stimulate and reinforce progress.

Many sources provide characteristics of effective schools, but most are too broad and try to encompass all facets of the school. That is not the intent here. In the discussion of traits and beliefs that follows, our purpose is to provide a lens for viewing characteristics that can be influenced by mathematics coaches—that is, those areas most directly related to teaching and learning.

THE PRESENT: TODAY'S MATHEMATICS CLASSROOMS

Since 1995, the National Center for Education Statistics, through the *Trends in International Mathematics and Science Study (TIMSS)*, has collected data on mathematics and science achievement of students in the United States and other countries. These studies provide a picture of what happens in many mathematics classrooms across this country, showing with some consistency how lessons are structured and how content is taught in many, if not most, U.S. schools. These characteristics, confirmed by additional research, can be used to paint the picture of the present when it comes to mathematics instruction.

Current Traits

Following are six traits most associated with mathematics instruction in today's classrooms. They predominate; they are not universal. But they are prevalent to a high degree and so can be seen to represent the present.

1. Teachers are the primary source of information.

Teachers assume that students know the mathematics they have been taught in prior classes but do not know other relevant information that will help them learn new methods and procedures. Teachers therefore add information, and students must make sense of it, properly filing it in the correct corner of their brains for future reference. Many teachers believe that "learning takes place primarily through memorization of facts and specific skills" (Caine & Caine, 1994, p. 4). The role of the teacher thus is to supply these facts and skills. The fastest, most expeditious way to cover the mathematics curriculum is by teachers sharing their knowledge.

Unfortunately, this is not the most effective method for learning. According to Jensen (1998), "Teachers who continue to emphasize one-sided lecture methods are violating an important principle of our brain: Essentially we are social beings and our brains grow in a social environment" (p. 93).

By dominating the classroom conversation and limiting student input, teachers are able to cover more material and maintain classroom control. They also are better able to schedule, predict, and regulate their time.

2. Students are passive listeners.

Being busy or quiet is not the same as being engaged. Students receive instruction on mathematics methods and procedures and are expected to replicate processes when asked to do so. Mathematics classrooms are arranged to reinforce a lecture-based, information-giving approach to teaching and learning. Students are seated at desks in neat rows positioned so that they can maintain eye contact with the teacher. The front of the room is the center of attention. Students are expected to listen and learn. Questions tend to be asked by teachers rather than students, and the intent of these questions is for students to provide brief, knowledge-level answers. This style of interaction allows the teacher to control the flow of information. This approach persists as the common instructional style in classrooms. The NRC (2001) has named it "recitation"—a running dialogue of fill-in-the-blank-type discussion.

3. Instruction follows rigid methodology.

A rigid instructional structure has developed in schools because of the first two traits. The hallmark document for capturing the current state of mathematics classrooms in the United States and several other countries has become TIMSS (Trends in Mathematics and Science Study, or more commonly Third International Mathematics and Science Study), which has been administered at four-year intervals since 1995. The study reports typify instruction in mathematics classrooms as lecture and skill practice. The subject area is covered, and the primary resource is an adopted textbook. Student engagement in the learning process is minimal. A consistent pattern of teaching appears to include the following features:

- a review of previous material and homework;
- a problem illustration by the teacher;
- drill on low-level procedures that imitate those demonstrated by the teacher;
- supervised seat work by students, often in isolation;
- checking of seat work problems; and
- assignment of homework. (National Commission on Mathematics and Science Teaching for the 21st Century, 2000, p. 20)

Strong evidence from TIMSS suggests that this instructional style is not effective for a majority of students; however, significant change in instructional strategies and methods has not yet occurred. Thompson (2003) captures the status quo:

For all of the fluidity and dynamism of school districts as social systems, the fundamental features of their underlying culture and structure tend to be stubbornly inert. It's a well-known fact that the modern public school and the school district are direct descendants of the Industrial Revolution. Public schools were modeled after factories, and factories were built to last. Factories have traditionally been designed with an eye toward optimizing efficiency through regimented processes. A blood relative of such regimentation is aversion to change. (p. 489)

Short and Greer (2002) concur that reform efforts must continue with a goal of breaking the grip of the factory model.

4. The textbook is the curriculum.

In this pervasive instructional model, the textbook is the primary source of teacher materials. Textbook publishers find themselves in a dilemma. If they deviate from this prevalent instructional pattern, then teachers may not adopt their textbooks. Even when publishers know and can introduce more effective, inclusive instructional strategies and approaches, they dare not do so. Marzano (2003) notes,

> One of the major findings from the Third International Mathematics and Science Study (TIMSS) was that teachers in the United States exhibited an over-reliance on textbooks for decisions about content and pacing (Stevenson and Stigler 1992, Stigler and Hiebert 1999). If textbooks were organized in ways consistent with known principles of learning, this wouldn't be so bad. (p. 107)

This overreliance on textbooks continues to dominate instructional practice and reinforces students' understanding that mathematics is mostly memorization and procedure.

5. Assessments are procedural.

Assessments reflect mathematical procedures practiced during instruction. The textbook, as the primary resource, provides students with ample opportunities to practice procedures. In a typical lesson, teachers show students how to complete steps in finding the solution to a problem. Students then practice until they are proficient in the skill. Assessments are drawn from the textbook and reflect the exact skill in the format that students have practiced.

This style of assessment is reinforced by the use of scanning machines. With procedural skills, only correct answers are sought. This provides the opportunity to use multiple-choice tests in which students carry out algorithms and calculations, locate correct answers, and bubble-in answer choices. Students see what is tested and how it is tested as indicators of what is important and valued. Thus, they quickly learn that mathematics is merely procedural. Logically students' most routine question becomes, "Is this going to be on the test?"

6. Knowledge is recall.

The NRC (2005) provides an example of the marked discrepancy between research on learning and actual classroom practice:

Why are associations with mathematics so negative for so many people? If we look through the lens of *How People Learn*, we see a subject that is rarely taught in a way that makes use of the three principles that are the focus of this volume. Instead of connecting with, building on, and refining the mathematical understandings, intuitions, and resourcefulness that students bring to the classroom (Principle 1), mathematics instruction often overrides students' reasoning processes, replacing them with a set of rules and procedures that disconnects problem solving from meaning making. Instead of organizing the skills and competencies required to do mathematics fluently around a set of core mathematical concepts (Principle 2), those skills and competencies are often themselves the center, and sometimes the whole, of instruction. And precisely because the acquisition of procedural knowledge is often divorced from meaning making, students do not use metacognitive strategies (Principle 3) when they engage in solving mathematics problems. (p. 217)

These misconceptions about learning permeate current mathematics classrooms and serve as a challenge for mathematics coaches. Using the learning principles from the NRC, coaches can assess where a school or teachers stands philosophically and what beliefs support teaching in the present. This assessment can serve as a starting point from which to measure progress.

Underlying Beliefs

Certain underlying beliefs go hand in hand with classroom traits, and it is difficult, if not impossible, to say which came first. Did the beliefs create the system, or did the system create the beliefs? In either case, both need to change if students are to achieve at higher levels. Mathematics coaches must change both classroom traits and the beliefs that support them. Following are present beliefs in summary:

1. Mathematics is memorization and procedure.

In general teachers who currently teach mathematics learned under the current, age-old methodology of memorization and procedure, and many, if not most, teach as they learned.

2. Mathematics is a filtering system.

Mathematics has been part of a filtering-system approach in which students conform to expectations and learn only to a level of achievement that is largely predetermined. DuFour (2004) gives this example:

Historically, . . . children have been guaranteed only the right to attend school rather than the right to learn. In fact, the prevalent assumption that has driven public education throughout most of the history of the United States is that few students were capable of high levels of learning. (pp. 15–16)

When education systems began operating for the general population, the society was still mainly agrarian. Most students needed little education beyond limited reading and computation. Although this is no longer the reality, much of this philosophy persists.

3. Teachers have a minimal effect on learning.

The idea that students reach a predetermined level of achievement and are filtered out when they reach it resonates with the notion that teachers really make little difference beyond being disseminators of information. Many teachers still assume that students who can learn the material will do so, and those who cannot learn it will not. This idea was supported as late as 1966 in the so-called Coleman Report (Coleman et al., 1966), which found that schooling did not affect learning. Rather, student background did (Marzano, 2003).

In her recent groundbreaking work on mind-sets that defines them as either "fixed" or "growth," Dweck (2006) also discovered a prevalent idea among people with a fixed mind-set that supported the knowledge dissemination approach:

Either you have ability or you expend effort. . . . Effort is for those who don't have the ability. People with the fixed mindset tell us, "If you have to work at something, you must not be good at it." (p. 40)

These ideas have been refuted by recent research on how students learn, yet the beliefs persist. One of the jobs of mathematics coaches is to work toward dismantling these old beliefs and leading schools and teachers toward an understanding that all students can achieve to a high level though effective teaching and learning.

THE FUTURE: TOMORROW'S MATHEMATICS CLASSROOMS

In looking toward the future, mathematics coaches need a framework to guide envisioning desired classrooms. Developing a curriculum, designing lessons, and constructing classroom activities all will proceed from this common vision. The NRC (2001) developed such a framework and defined mathematical proficiency through five component parts:

- conceptual understanding—comprehension of mathematical concepts, operations, and relations;
- procedural fluency—skill in carrying out procedures flexibly, accurately, efficiently, and appropriately;
- strategic competence—ability to formulate, represent, and solve mathematical problems;
- adaptive reasoning—capacity for logical thought, reflection, explanation, and justification; and
- productive disposition—habitual inclination to see mathematics as sensible, useful, and worthwhile. (p. 116)

These five parts serve as common ground for dialogue between teachers and coaches. A well-designed, high-quality mathematics curriculum addresses each of these proficiencies.

To align with these proficiencies, the National Council of Teachers of Mathematics (NCTM) developed *Principles and Standards for School Mathematics* (2000), which also offers a vision of the classrooms of the future. NCTM envisions classrooms that provide all students "access to high-quality, engaging mathematics instruction" (p. 3). Students are challenged with high expectations for learning and achievement with appropriate accommodations to support them in this quest. The "curriculum is rich with opportunities for students to learn important mathematics concepts and procedures with understanding" (p. 3) by engaging students in challenging mathematical tasks supported by appropriate technology. Students are provided ample opportunities to make conjectures, explain their reasoning, and justify answers by communicating both in writing and orally.

The NRC proficiencies and NCTM's ideal classrooms contain the traits of the future classroom, and there are underlying beliefs that support these traits.

Future (Desired) Traits

The desired traits of envisioned, highly effective mathematics classrooms include the following:

1. Teachers are empowered.

The envisioned classrooms have empowered teachers who demonstrate learning through the performance of their students. Empowerment is a continuous loop. Teachers believe they can teach mathematics to students and so are willing to expend the time and energy needed to do so. When student performance demonstrates success, teachers feel a strong sense of accomplishment. This sense of accomplishment rejuvenates teachers, leads to additional efforts, and raises even higher expectations for student learning (Conzemius & O'Neill, 2001).

Empowered teachers set high expectations for learning and then find ways to help students meet them. Achievement is based on the belief that all students can learn at high levels. Research by Dweck (2006) on mind-sets reinforces this belief:

> But some teachers preached and practiced a growth mindset. They focused on the idea that all children could develop their skills, and in their classrooms a weird thing happened. It didn't matter whether students started the year in the high—or the low—ability group. Both groups ended the year way up high. (p. 66)

In classrooms staffed by empowered teachers, the students do learn mathematics. Evidence supporting the effect of classroom teachers on students' learning is overwhelming (Marzano, 2003; NRC, 2001; Stronge, 2007). Mathematics coaches are strong allies in the empowerment process.

2. Curriculum is implemented as designed.

Opportunity to learn the established curriculum is a fundamental tenet of achieving equity, closing achievement gaps, and ensuring student success in learning mathematics (English, 2000; Marzano, 2003). The alignment between the intended curriculum, the implemented curriculum, and the attained curriculum—often described as the written, the taught, and the tested—is crucial for mathematics coaches to understand and address. Far too often alignment is assumed or taken on faith, and this is perhaps the most serious mistake mathematics coaches can make in working to improve student achievement. Conzemius and O'Neill (2001) state the obvious but necessary: "We also know that children who have the opportunity to learn the content they will be tested on score higher than children who don't learn the material beforehand" (p. 57). Curriculum misalignment is cumulative over years of instruction and most seriously harms students who depend on schools most for all of their learning needs—the traditionally underserved.

The mathematics curriculum also must match state-identified content knowledge and process skills. With alignment among all contributors—classroom, school, district, and state—mathematics coaches are positioned to ensure that the mathematics curriculum is delivered as designed.

3. Multiple instructional strategies are employed.

Students learn in different ways. Effective teachers clearly understand this and do something about it. Teachers also understand that students are social beings and that talking is a powerful learning tool. To accommodate these understandings and to increase student learning, teachers use multiple instructional strategies, including individual, small-group, and whole-group approaches (Stronge, 2007).

4. Students are actively engaged.

For students to learn to high levels, they must be engaged in the learning activities. The greater the individual student's level of engagement, the higher the degree of learning (Dweck, 2006; NRC, 2004a). The relationship between engagement and learning crosses all student groups—"whether students are rich or poor, black, brown, or white" (NRC, 2004a, p. 1). Actively engaged students are gathering data, running experiments, testing ideas, exploring, postulating, and justifying their reasoning and solutions to challenging problems. Students are talking to members of their group, to study partners, and to teachers. The classroom is buzzing with a productive hum—all about mathematics.

5. Assessment is varied.

One of the many challenges to teachers is to make assessments of learning valuable to students. Feedback on learning is important to students, and, when done appropriately, promotes their involvement in setting learning goals and participating fully in learning activities. To accomplish this end, assessments need to be reexamined. The NRC (2000) says, "The roles of assessment must be expanded beyond the traditional concept of testing. The use of frequent formative assessment helps make students' thinking visible to themselves, their peers, and their teacher" (p. 19).

In order to make thinking visible, assessments need to be varied in design. For example, short multiple-choice tests can quickly identify potential problem areas for teachers and students to address. Other assessments should require students to record their thinking as they work to solve problems. These open-ended assessments allow teachers and students to identify conceptual understandings and misunderstandings. Other types of assessments can give students opportunities to share what they know about a topic rather than highlighting what they do not know.

Assessment is more than a Friday test or quiz. Assessment is both formal, as described above, and informal. As students are more actively engaged in learning activities, teachers have a greater opportunity to check in with them. As teachers move about the classroom, they listen to students' conversations and observe their work. Such informal assessment is possible only when students are engaged by motivating activities and working with their peers.

Underlying Beliefs

Desired, or future, traits are part of a system of underlying beliefs, including the following:

1. All students can learn.

In effective schools and classrooms, the belief that all students can learn is continually expressed and proven to be true. Teachers believe that mathematics is a valuable skill to be learned and that students can learn it to high levels (Stronge, 2007). When confronted with students who are not being successful, teachers do not look for excuses but take steps to intervene. Regardless of students' backgrounds or experiences in mathematics, teachers hold students to high standards and help the students reach them (Dweck, 2006).

2. Teachers can teach the students.

The firm, unshakable belief that all students can successfully learn mathematics is linked to another belief, knowing that teachers can teach students. Teachers design classroom activities to teach students mathematics. How well these activities are designed and presented determines to a large extent the success of students' learning (Kennedy, 2005).

Teachers have a tremendous influence on student learning. Engaged and engaging teachers promote student confidence. Students believe that they can learn mathematics and that they can learn it from their teacher (NRC, 2004a). Students quickly sense teachers' enthusiasm for their subject, become enthused, and decide they want to learn (Stronge, 2007).

3. Mathematics is conceptual and developmental.

Mathematics is rooted in conceptual understanding. These concepts develop as students encounter higher levels of mathematics as they progress through grades and courses. Mathematics is not a set of rules and procedures that are memorized and discarded with the introduction of each number system, moving from natural numbers to integers to rational numbers and then to real numbers.

Meaningful understandings and information retention mean that students connect new learning to previous learning (Loucks-Horsley et al., 2003). Students need help making such connections. Teachers assist students to recall prior understandings and then provide opportunities to make sense of new content through self-assessment and reflection (NRC, 1999).

CRITICAL POINTS

Improving mathematics achievement means moving every classroom teacher from the present to the future. This is a significant change, and to make it happen, mathematics coaches must understand both what today's classrooms look like and what tomorrow's classrooms *should* look like.

Two short assessments (Figures 2.1 and 2.2) follow that will be helpful in furthering coaches' understandings of current and desired classrooms. Each provides a snapshot of classroom actions. Mathematics coaches should complete both forms by visiting classrooms or drawing from personal experiences. The completed forms should then be compared side by side. The scales are reversed so that coaches can quickly see trends. If circled responses trend to the right side of the page on both forms, then the classrooms are more traditional ("present") in their approach to mathematics teaching. If the circled responses on both forms trend to the left side, then the classrooms are more envisioned and desired ("future").

Figure 2.1   Assessment of Classroom Status: Current

Complete this form by visiting classrooms or drawing from personal experiences.
Circle one response for each item.

Teachers are the primary source of information:

Teachers are talking.	rarely occasionally often usually
Teachers are in front.	rarely occasionally often usually
Questions are closed-ended.	rarely occasionally often usually

Students are passive listeners:

Desks are in rows.	rarely occasionally often usually
Students talk only to the teacher.	rarely occasionally often usually
Students work independently.	rarely occasionally often usually

Instruction follows rigid methodology:

Lesson flow is predicable.	rarely occasionally often usually
Lessons are consistent from day to day.	rarely occasionally often usually

Textbook is the curriculum:

Students have textbooks open.	rarely occasionally often usually
Teacher materials are textbook.	rarely occasionally often usually
Samples are from textbook.	rarely occasionally often usually

Assessments are procedural:

Tests are given weekly.	rarely occasionally often usually
Tests are from textbook.	rarely occasionally often usually
Tests are multiple choice.	rarely occasionally often usually

Knowledge is recall:

Student responses are short.	rarely occasionally often usually
Questions are at knowledge level.	rarely occasionally often usually

Figure 2.2 Assessment of Classroom Status: Desired

Complete this form by visiting classrooms or drawing from personal experiences. Circle one response for each item.

Teachers are empowered:

Teachers display enthusiasm.	usually	often	occasionally	rarely
Teachers ask open-ended questions.	usually	often	occasionally	rarely
Teachers promote high expectations.	usually	often	occasionally	rarely

Curriculum is implemented as designed:

District documents are evident.	usually	often	occasionally	rarely
Various materials are used.	usually	often	occasionally	rarely
Lesson objectives are clear.	usually	often	occasionally	rarely

Multiple strategies are employed:

Activities are challenging.	usually	often	occasionally	rarely
Activities are hands-on/experimental.	usually	often	occasionally	rarely
Student desks are moved.	usually	often	occasionally	rarely

Students are engaged:

Students talk to students.	usually	often	occasionally	rarely
Students work in groups.	usually	often	occasionally	rarely
Students discuss thinking.	usually	often	occasionally	rarely
Students are productive.	usually	often	occasionally	rarely

Assessments are varied:

Students show work.	usually	often	occasionally	rarely
Students write explanations.	usually	often	occasionally	rarely
Assessment types change.	usually	often	occasionally	rarely

3 Building Rapport With Teachers

The three chapters in Part I are devoted to preparing a foundation for mathematics coaching. In Chapter 1 we defined *mathematics coach* and examined the roles, skills, and characteristics of mathematics coaches. In Chapter 2 we described mathematics classrooms in terms of present realities, based on studies and assessments such as TIMSS, and an envisioned future of desired traits and underlying beliefs. In this final chapter of Part I we turn to a fundamental process element, namely, building rapport. To be successful, mathematics coaches must build rapport with the teachers they coach.

Rapport with teachers is a necessary building block to attain the goal of improved mathematics achievement for every student. Building rapport means establishing a collegial, professional working relationship with the specific purpose of providing continuous effective learning opportunities for teachers. Good rapport establishes an environment in which this can be achieved. A collaborative relationship enables a coach to help teachers develop deep mathematical content knowledge and effective, research-based instructional strategies. Rapport equates to trust, developed through positive relationships experienced over time. With rapport, a mathematics coach can communicate to teachers how and why changing and improving instruction makes a difference in student learning, and support from a mathematics coach helps teachers to deliver consistently successful lessons.

HOW TO BUILD RAPPORT

There is no magic recipe for building rapport, but there are steps that coaches can take, including the following:

Be professionally friendly.

Make a connection with teachers. A key point is to validate teachers as professional colleagues. Help teachers understand that the coach's role is to support them in implementing best practices and reaching their school's or district's student achievement goals. Help teachers feel important and look for ways to praise the work they do. Maintain a positive, optimistic view to create a bond and to inspire teachers to try new instructional strategies that have been proven to enhance students' learning. Celebrate positive changes, however small. Give credit for successes and changes to teachers. Giving credit does wonders in promoting collegiality and collaboration. And, finally, find opportunities to ask questions and learn about teachers' backgrounds, because information about past experiences can be useful in developing future strategies to help them help their students.

Be persistent, visible, and accessible.

Teachers want and need predictability. Mistrust comes when teachers do not know what to expect. Always fulfill promises and keep appointments so that teachers will know the coach is dependable. Be visible and accessible to support teachers' needs as curricular and instructional changes are being implemented. Communicate often. Regular encouragement will assure teachers that their time and effort are appreciated. And, of course, be patient, because changes take time.

Listen respectfully.

Teachers will appreciate, respect, and value a mathematics coach who is a good listener. Analyze what teachers say and ask clarification questions. Be aware of body language and facial expressions—both of teachers and coaches. Confirm understanding by paraphrasing. For example, one way to respond is to begin with, "What I think I heard you say . . ." And certainly avoid interruptions.

Keep confidences.

Teachers may be reluctant to share their fears and concerns when discussing strengths and weaknesses. They will confide in a coach who is discreet and can be relied on to maintain confidentiality. If a teacher believes that a coach is talking about them to other teachers, parents, or administrators, then trust will be lost. Trust is at the heart of coaching, because trust is an important enabler for teachers to be willing to try new approaches and unfamiliar instructional strategies.

Maintain content knowledge.

A mathematics coach should have a rich mathematical background of content knowledge, from number theory and measurement to algebra and geometry to probability and data analysis. Up-to-date content knowledge must be complemented by a sound and varied repertoire of instructional strategies readily available to share with teachers based on their individual needs.

Give teachers choices.

Often mathematics coaches know what needs to be done first, but they can gain teachers' cooperation by providing choices of initial steps toward change. For example, if student data show that improvement is needed in content knowledge in algebra and geometry, the coach might let the teacher choose which to work on first. Another kind of choice might be to permit teachers to choose times for collaborative meetings and feedback conferences, choose which classes the coach is to visit, or perhaps choose among various instructional strategies to implement initially. Giving choices helps teachers understand that they still have control over what takes place in their classrooms.

Stay on task.

Rapport establishes a collegial relationship based on mutual respect. Rapport amounts to an unwritten contract between coaches and teachers. But it may fall to the coaches to ensure that progress toward change and improvement is maintained as the primary purpose for this relationship. Professional friendship cannot be allowed to divert attention from the goal of improved teaching and learning.

Stay in touch.

Part of good communication is staying in touch when face-to-face meetings are not available. Correspond with teachers and administrators to keep them informed about new and promising practices. This ensures a common body of knowledge and a shared vocabulary. Provide reminders of common learning goals for student success, thus enabling teachers to improve their confidence in discussing learning issues with colleagues and leaders.

Look for teachable moments.

Rapport also can be built by giving teachers information—content or strategies—they need immediately. When a need is noticed or expressed, that is a teachable moment. Immediate feedback or interaction increases teachers' confidence in a coach's competence.

COACHING SCENARIOS

Building rapport with teachers is a complex undertaking. It is achieved over a period of time, not through a single event but a connected series of events. Some of these events may be brief, while others may occur in steps or stages. Following are three scenarios that will be helpful in further understanding how coaches build rapport. Questions are provided throughout so that you may reflect on the steps of each scenario.

SCENARIO 1: THE RESISTANT MIDDLE-LEVEL TEACHER

Following is the situation:

> A veteran seventh-grade teacher told a newly hired coach that mathematics coaching services were not wanted and definitely not needed. This middle school teacher of 25 years further indicated that her retirement was soon approaching; therefore, changes in instruction would not occur. This teacher ultimately refused to attend any "useless" professional development sessions.

First, the questions: What should the coach do? Which of the previously listed steps could the coach take in this situation? How can the coach build rapport with a teacher who truthfully says that she does not believe in mathematics coaching? How can the coach establish a positive relationship with a teacher who will be asked to change how she teaches in order to teach in ways congruent with desired teaching practice? How can the coach reach a teacher who does not see ongoing professional learning as a teacher's responsibility to ensure student success?

Coaching Considerations

Some perceptions may be helpful to consider. For example, the resistant teacher's behavior may be the result of insecurity or simply fear of change. To be observed by a mathematics coach who might uncover what is really happening in the classroom might be stressful for this (or any) teacher. She may see the mathematics coach as coming into her classroom to change everything all at once, which would be frightening. She also may see the mathematics coach as an evaluator sent by the administration. Finally, being observed by a mathematics coach may be worrisome to any teacher who does not understand that the focus of professional learning is improving students' thinking, learning, and achievement. A mathematics coach must recognize the emotional effort that this or any teacher must expend in order to change.

The mathematics coach responded to the teacher in this way:

"I think it is wonderful that you are a pro and have been teaching for many years. You have a background of experience that encompasses 25 years. I bet you could write a book on all the changes you have witnessed over the years. I personally think it is exciting to learn about research-based practices that really will make a difference in student learning. It will be so good to get to know you better and find out what ideas you have used and what has been successful for you.

"By the way, job-embedded learning is something you will like; it won't be useless. It is true that in past years teachers have been subjected to professional development through one-shot, one-day inservice workshops. Onetime training led by a workshop leader usually lacks continuity and may not be guided by a coherent, ongoing plan integrated with district or school improvement goals. Studies show that after attending such a workshop teachers remember less than 15% of what they learned and implement less than 7% of the new learning. But we are not going to do that. We are going to have a continuous-learning focus that will build knowledge over time.

"I know we can implement positive change through collaborating. We are going to start by looking at student data. What time may I come visit your classroom tomorrow? I am so very pleased to work with you as your mathematics coach. I can't wait to see you tomorrow."

Which steps toward building rapport did the mathematics coach use? Here is how the scenario continued:

The mathematics teacher was stunned when she was asked to choose the time for the observation. Selecting her highest-performing math class, she was sure the mathematics coach would be pleased with the instruction taking place with gifted prealgebra students. During the coach's initial classroom visit, the teacher introduced the lesson, and the students quickly caught on mechanically and procedurally. The teacher then assigned 50 homework problems for the students to practice silently on their own. The teacher sat behind her desk to grade papers. The teacher ignored the mathematics coach and did not introduce the coach to the students.

What should the mathematics coach do in this circumstance?

Coaching Considerations

Obviously, time is needed to win trust; there are no shortcuts. In the first visit to the classroom, the mathematics coach must find and communicate something the teacher does well. In this case of the middle-level teacher, a word wall of vocabulary terms decoratively lined the bulletin board at the front of the room. The bulletin board was visually appealing and contained terms that the students needed to learn for the state assessment test.

The scenario continued in this manner:

The hour-long classroom visit ended with the mathematics coach writing a note and handing it to the teacher. The note read: "There may be close to 500 mathematics terms that students need to know by the time they enroll in high school. You have created a visually appealing word wall that is an awesome resource for helping students remember and master mathematics vocabulary. The other day I saw another tool you might be interested in using. It is called the Frayer vocabulary model. May I share this model with you the next time we meet? What would you think about coplanning a lesson together?"

Unfortunately, the teacher quipped that no time for planning was available. She decided to use lesson plans from the previous year, even though assessment data had revealed students' lack of mastery. The teacher indicated she had never reflected on the lessons she taught, again stating that time was a major issue.

Again, the teacher was proving resistant, in this instance using perceived lack of time as a reason to resist the mathematics coach's overtures. Here is how the coach responded:

The mathematics coach acknowledged the teacher's busy schedule but suggested that thinking about how students learn is a powerful element of teaching. The teacher then asked the coach asked to explain the Frayer vocabulary model—quickly. To the mathematics coach's delight, after the short explanation the teacher asked what other mathematics vocabulary models existed. Just as with students, there are teachable moments for teachers. The coach seized the opportunity to demonstrate a variety of vocabulary strategies. In collaboration they made plans to focus on vocabulary strategies during upcoming units. The next day the mathematics coach sent the teacher a follow-up e-mail that provided a research-based explanation of the Frayer vocabulary model and other models.

Again, it will be useful to pause and consider the rapport-building steps that the coach took. This is what happened next:

Teachers usually want to talk about themselves and their experiences. In asking questions during the dialogue that took place about vocabulary strategies, the mathematics coach discovered the teacher had taken an online course with the intent to be certified in mathematics at the middle level. However, because of time conflicts, she dropped the program and was not endorsed, certified, or licensed to teach middle-level mathematics. The teacher also believed that checking and grading papers was taking up valuable afterschool time.

But then came another teachable moment. The coach engaged the teacher in a discussion about the purpose of grading papers and providing student feedback. The teacher believed grading was for report cards only. She saw no interim diagnostic value. The teacher had never learned about providing useful feedback through guided practice with active student responses, exit quizzes, or mathematics journals, all of which can eliminate long evenings of grading papers.

As a result of this teachable moment, the coach also decided that more information about guided practice could be useful to the other teachers. The coach approached the administration and requested an opportunity to present a professional learning session on guided practice for all teachers at a future meeting.

Once more, consider the rapport-building steps that the mathematics coach took in the one-on-one contacts with the resistant teacher.

In summary, the mathematics coach focused on instructional strategies initially. It was apparent from the classroom visit that the teacher did not have a large repertoire of successful teaching strategies. Lecturing with little student involvement seemed to be her dominant strategy. Discovery learning was not used, nor were the teacher's questioning techniques particularly effective.

With time, the coach and this initially resistant teacher built a successful professional relationship. Finding planning time was a continual struggle. There were many interruptions during the teacher's planning time, including unannounced visits from parents, school assemblies or programs, and weather-related interruptions. Many feedback conferences were only 15 minutes long. But as time passed the mathematics teacher found ways to sneak in more collaborative planning time. On one occasion the prealgebra class was combined with another teacher's class, and in another instance the principal volunteered to teach a class in order to give the coach and teacher time to meet.

Change is a process, not an event. As teachers come to value what they are learning and as their personal needs are met, they often become creative at finding ways to meet and truly want to continue the collaboration with the mathematics coach.

SCENARIO 2: THE FEARFUL FIRST-YEAR TEACHER

Following is another situation to consider from the standpoint of building rapport:

An elementary school teacher contacted the mathematics coach for help. Early in the school year, this novice teacher taught a lesson about decimal place values from the textbook. Her fourth-grade students did not do well on their assignment from the book, and all failed the test at the end of the chapter. Her fourth-grade colleagues suggested that this first-year teacher copy extra practice worksheets, make a stapled packet of them for additional drill, and send them home with her students, rather than spend more class time on the subject matter.

The teacher seemed panicky in her dialogue with the mathematics coach, making several fearful comments, such as, "I'm afraid I will get fired if my students don't do well on the state assessment, and this decimal place value objective will be tested. The other fourth-grade teachers told me I can't spend another day on this topic. I must follow a long-range pacing calendar that tells me what to teach each day. Subtraction with decimals is the objective I need to be teaching today, not place value. What should I do? I really need your help. Math is a very difficult subject for me to teach. I am just not very good in math."

First, the questions: What should the coach do? Which steps might the coach use in this situation to build rapport with this fearful first-year teacher? What advice would help calm the teacher and help her lead her students to mastery of the content that has challenged them?

Coaching Considerations

A mathematics coach who wants to build rapport with teachers must empathize with them. In this case the coach must understand the new teacher's frustrations and simultaneously get at the root of the learning problem. The coach must be a learning leader and guide the teacher toward learning and using best practices. Thus, discussions between the coach and the teacher will need to focus on student assessment data, instructional strategies such as decimal place value models, and best practices with regard to assigning homework.

This is what the mathematics coach said to the teacher:

"I think I heard you say that you are afraid of being fired. Many new teachers fear the unknown, but today you made a decision to seek help. I am really glad you called. Please know that I want to be of service and support you during your first year. It is not possible to teach every lesson perfectly the first year of teaching. We will tackle the issues together. It will be several months before your administrator decides on your status, so you don't need to worry about being fired at this time. Worrying is like a rocking chair; you go back and forth and don't get anywhere. We are going to start with the chapter assessment to look at your students' results and then move forward, never backward. Just so you know, I don't think you would find any teacher who has not retaught a lesson that did not go well."

What steps did the mathematics coach take to build rapport with this teacher?

The scenario continued:

The teacher smiled at the reference to a rocking chair and seemed to relax, knowing she was not alone. Before any further discussion could take place, the teacher mentioned that a few parents had complained about the assigned 10-page packet that she had sent home with a due date of the next school day. Four parents had called the school and spoken with the principal, who passed the calls on to the teacher.

The mathematics coach noted that this was the perfect basis for a discussion about ongoing communication with parents and realistic homework expectations. But before that discussion, another was necessary. This is what the mathematics coach said:

> "You said the students all failed the chapter test. Instead of focusing solely on low test scores, why don't we look at the actual tests to determine specifically what students know and what you may need to reteach? Let's flip through the exams and see what you notice. And let's record what you see."

The coach also addressed the teacher's fear about pacing:

> "Some teachers I know use a pretest to establish a focus for a textbook chapter. There may be several objectives that your students already know. You may be able simply to review these objectives with your learners versus spending two or three days as the plan suggests. That may help you catch up with the long-range pacing calendar. By the way, you already know that it is important for your students to make sense of what they are learning, rather that just drilling with repetitive practice for the state assessment. After all, your students will need to apply their knowledge in real-life situations. The long-range pacing plan is merely a blueprint or a guide to help you prepare students for the state assessment. You are in charge in this classroom, and you are the only one who knows at this point what your students are capable of doing. You are the expert with your students. If an additional day is needed to develop the understanding of decimal place value, use that day wisely."

Again, what are the steps that the coach used to build rapport? Following is how this scenario concluded:

> The first-year teacher had not acquired an adequate background to teach elementary mathematics. Her content knowledge was weak, and she did not use appropriate instructional strategies. Through several conversations the mathematics coach discovered that the first-year teacher had student-taught with an elementary teacher who did not like teaching mathematics. Her mentor had provided mathematics instruction for only 20 minutes at the end of each day and then sent home numerous mathematics practice pages for homework, creating a situation where parents were forced to do the real teaching. This student-teaching experience did not provide a good model for the first-year teacher.

The coach pointed out that every teacher must be a lifelong learner and pay attention to research-based practices that are proven to work for teaching mathematics. The focus of coaching sessions over time was on effective manipulatives and models. This focus not only improved the teacher's knowledge of instructional strategies but also increased her content knowledge. The coach and the teacher met regularly to preview coming chapters and to learn about numbers, algebra, geometry, measurement, and data. The teacher's fears and frustrations abated, and her students scored well on the state mathematics assessment. The teacher became an asset to the school district.

Coaching Considerations

First-year teachers often leave the profession out of fear and frustration. In this scenario, job-embedded learning with the mathematics coach may well be credited for helping an unprepared, fearful newcomer receive the support she needed to stay in the profession. The school district in this case also realized that building rapport and confidence was important to a new teacher's success.

Another factor helped set the stage for coaching success. All of the teachers in the district attended a summer orientation to the school district's goals and expectations. The mathematics coach was introduced, and the coach's role was explained. This turned out to be an initial rapport-building activity, which encouraged the new teacher to accept coaching. The teacher was willing to share her concerns. And this willingness helped the coach identify key issues and design an approach that met the teacher's needs.

SCENARIO 3: THE HIGH SCHOOL TEACHER WHO HID THE CURRICULUM

Following is the last of our three scenarios about building rapport:

A high school mathematics teacher, greatly respected by her colleagues, held the title of department chair. In a conversation with the mathematics coach, this teacher commented about several disruptive 10th-grade students who consistently misbehaved during the lectures in her Algebra I class. Almost daily the teacher sent these students into the hallway or to the principal's office with discipline referrals.

The students, she reported, were put into in-school suspension and were falling behind with mathematics assignments. The teacher who monitored in-school suspension was not a mathematics teacher and could not help these students with their assignments. If the students could not complete their work, they would surely fail the class and would not be allowed to enroll in the next course, Algebra II. Without these courses the students also would not be prepared for the high-stakes state assessment administered in the 11th grade. The solution this teacher and her colleagues determined was that the mathematics coach should tutor these students.

As in the previous scenarios, first the questions: What should the coach do? Which steps in building rapport could be used in this situation? How can rapport be built with a department chair teacher who convinces her mathematics colleagues that the coach should conduct a tutoring program for disruptive students? How might a relationship be built with a teacher who specifically wants the coach to provide students with repetitive drill?

Coaching Considerations

The teacher is legitimately concerned about the 10th-grade students missing daily instruction and potentially not doing well on the state assessment. It appears that the curriculum is being hidden from the students, because they are not being taught nor are they learning on their own what they need to know. Dismissing students from the classroom seems like a solution that works for the teacher but may not be good for the students. The coach may need to help the teacher reflect on her instructional practices. Is lecturing the best way for these students to learn? Are there other teaching strategies that could be used to involve the students actively? Are there motivation techniques that the teacher could try to keep these students in the mathematics class?

Following is how the mathematics coach responded:

"I understand you and your colleagues have talked about what to do with disruptive students sent out of mathematics classes. I know that you are deeply concerned that your students are not learning and won't be prepared for the assessment test next year. I know from our conversation that you and your colleagues feel the best approach for this issue is a tutorial class. However, my job description will not allow me to do this. What I can do is coplan with you and coteach with you in your classroom. I also can be supportive to the other teachers. May I visit your second period and then meet with you in your planning time during fourth period?"

The teacher replied, "Yeah, but you will see that the kids should not be in the class. Their behavior is awful. If you stay for third period, you will see that the students are perfectly behaved."

What steps did the mathematics coach take to build rapport with this teacher?

Coaching Considerations

As it turned out, the teacher was correct in her prediction about the second-period class. Student behavior was appalling, and the mathematics coach watched students being sent out of the classroom. The mathematics coach also noted that the teacher lectured for 20 minutes. Whenever a student raised a hand to ask a question, the teacher said, "Not now, I will answer individual questions in a few minutes when I am finished talking."

Over the course of the class period, the coach jotted down several important observations:

- The teacher was not actively involving students in their learning.
- Misbehaving students were social learners whose needs were not being met.
- Students would benefit from cooperative learning situations in which they could make sense of what was supposed to be learned.
- The teacher was in front of the classroom doing all the work, expecting students to follow along and then practice in silence.
- The pullout tutorial program would have met the teacher's need. The teacher would not need to put up with the bad behavior if the students weren't in the room.

According to the teacher, the third period was a dream class. From the standpoint of quiet orderliness, the mathematics coach found that to be true. Students in the third-period advanced algebra/trig class were attentive during the 20-minute lecture, and when the assignment was given, all of the students worked on their own. The students raised their hands if they needed help.

What should the coach do? What steps will build rapport with this teacher so that the mathematics coach can introduce the teacher to new strategies that will change how students respond to her teaching?

This is how the scenario played out:

The high school teacher truly believed that the misbehaving students should be kicked out of the class for the rest of the year. She believed her job was to impart information and teach the mathematics textbook. If the students chose to learn, that was great, but if they didn't, she should not have to put up with them. Someone else could teach them.

The mathematics coach mentioned that assessment data confirmed that the students were appropriately placed in the correct mathematics class, and no learning issues had been reported in prior years. The coach suggested that the teacher try a few new teaching strategies before making a major decision to transfer the students out of her class. The coach and teacher decided together that the second-period class should be videotaped. The coach promised the camera would not focus on the teacher but on the students. But the microphone also recorded the teacher teaching the lesson.

Together the coach and teacher analyzed the video to determine how to help the students. On observing the students in the video, the teacher commented on the students' body language and then immediately said, "They didn't understand because they weren't listening. Did I talk too long?" A discussion followed with the teacher agreeing to plan a lesson the next day with her coteaching partner, the mathematics coach. The "aha!" moment of the video helped the high school teacher began to change some of her instructional practices.

These three scenarios portray mathematics coaches facing a few of the many types of challenges they encounter. In each of these cases, the situation did not deteriorate into a clash of wills or a power struggle. The coach did not run and complain to the principal. Instead, the coach began systematically building rapport. Developing rapport and a professional working relationship with teachers are key elements in successful mathematics coaching. None of these scenarios would have ended well if the teachers and coaches had not established a sense of trust and shared purpose.

These are not easy cases. They are real and were chosen for specific purposes. In Scenario 1 the coach faced an experienced but resistant teacher. Common ground was attained in mathematics content (through vocabulary) and coplanning opportunities. In Scenario 2 the coach worked with a first-year teacher weak in content knowledge. The approach was to strengthen planning, which also had a positive effect of strengthening the teacher's mathematics content knowledge. In Scenario 3 the coach worked with the department chair on fundamental beliefs about teaching and discipline. Again, the path to change was helping this teacher plan more effective lessons by viewing and analyzing the lessons she had been delivering.

Mathematics coaches need a place to start that will make a difference for teachers and their students. In these scenarios a coach could easily have gotten lost in the challenge. If coaches become so busy dealing with individual issues, then they risk losing sight of the big ideas of change—building rapport, focusing on content, strengthening planning, and so forth. The goal of this book is to ensure that coaches have the grounding they need to make change happen.

Part II of this book presents a Mathematics Coaching Model with chapters devoted to building on the principles and practices presented in Part I.

CRITICAL POINTS

The effectiveness of mathematics coaches is directly related to the degree to which coaches can foster strong, professional working relationships with teachers. Building rapport with teachers is a complex undertaking and can be achieved only over time. Rapport is a necessary building block to attain the goal of improved mathematics achievement for every student, because it establishes an environment in which this can be achieved.

Part II

Mathematics Coaching Model

4 Focusing on the Curriculum

Curriculum is the first step in the Mathematics Coaching Model. Teaching to identified state standards is one of the basic tenets of school improvement and for closing the achievement gap between student subgroups.

Alignment of the written, taught, and tested curricula is the cornerstone for success in student achievement (English, 2000). Marzano, in his 2003 book, *What Works in Schools: Translating Research into Action*, notes that education research strongly indicates that a "guaranteed and viable" curriculum is the major factor in successful schools. He defines *guaranteed* as the absolute assurance that district objectives are taught in every classroom by every teacher. He defines *viable* as the assurance that objectives can be taught in the allotted time. These two elements provide a necessary foundation for student access to mathematics content.

According to English (2000), a curriculum is any document supplied by a school or school district that defines the work of the teachers with regard to content to be taught and methods to be used. Two distinct areas in which coaches need to have knowledge emerge from this explanation: content and methods. A *curriculum content document* is used to describe the mathematics content and includes scope, sequence, and a time line. This document is based on state standards and could even be the state standards as written, if the state has so designed them.

A *curriculum methods guide* is more comprehensive than a curriculum content document. This guide includes information in the content document but also provides methods of instruction, including lesson designs and materials.

If there is a need to adapt or organize state standards to meet local requirements, then district staff must produce a curriculum content document.

Regardless of the locally adopted mathematics curriculum, teachers need to identify and highlight state-identified content. Teachers must make sure that the appropriate content is presented in the material they intend to teach, thus ensuring opportunity to learn. It is worthwhile for teachers to study state standards and ensure that required content is contained in the curriculum methods guide that they will use. In addition, the content must be presented to the correct depth, introduced developmentally, and allotted sufficient time—in other words, in a way that adheres to the established scope, sequence, and timeline.

WHY WORK TOWARD CURRICULUM ALIGNMENT?

Creating a curriculum methods guide from scratch, while perhaps a noble cause, is difficult at best and in most cases practically impossible. To produce aligned, comprehensive lessons that use highly effective instructional strategies and techniques takes years of work by teams of curriculum developers. The more that effective strategies and techniques are present in the adopted program, the easier the development of a content document and a methods guide will be. Mathematics coaches and instructional leaders need to start with the document and guide they have and begin planning how to improve them.

The hazard is this: When teachers are encouraged, or allowed by default, to select the mathematics content they will teach, true opportunity to learn can be ignored, and inequity often results. Students who are socioeconomically poorer and academically weaker tend to get less experienced teachers (Love, 2002). Teachers who are not confident in their teaching skills and mathematics knowledge will dilute the curriculum both in terms of content offered and strategies used. Opportunity to learn is important for all students, but for students whose only resource is the public school classroom, it is directly related to their quality of life. Diminished opportunity to learn results in students falling behind and subsequently being taught an even more diluted curriculum. The downward spiral wreaks havoc on achievement among students in the greatest need.

To begin the improvement effort, mathematics coaches should be primarily concerned with a viable mathematics curriculum aligned to state standards. Regardless of the current status of the curriculum, instructional leaders, especially coaches, are responsible for improving student achievement. Marzano's (2003) "viable" curriculum is a logical place to start.

Anyone involved in writing a curriculum content document must carefully study state standards and use them as the foundation for this document. The state standards must be arranged into a scope and sequence chart or plan before additional local objectives are included. Teachers often, of necessity, use a textbook as the basis for instructional strategies and materials. This approach is difficult to overcome; however, it perpetuates achievement gaps. If the adopted mathematics textbook must be used as the primary source of strategies and materials, then the standards can be used as a framework and at least content alignment can be ensured and progress made toward improvement. It is a starting point.

A curriculum aligned to state standards gives students equitable opportunities to learn. Using an aligned curriculum increases student achievement and teachers' sense of efficacy. Consistency in content delivery must be ensured regardless of which teacher a student is assigned to. This consistency can only be ensured when a clearly articulated, rigorous curriculum is identified and implemented—major job responsibilities of mathematics coaches.

No curriculum content document can be viewed as perfect and unchangeable. It is a living document that should be revised and improved based on evidence from the classroom and sound education research. Curriculum method guides likely will take a number of years to create. For this reason, later in this chapter we offer three methods (labeled A, B, and C) as ways to approach curriculum alignment.

CHALLENGING LESSONS IMPLEMENT THE CURRICULUM

In leading the implementation of an aligned curriculum, mathematics coaches work to create challenging lessons. In collaborating with teachers to develop such lessons, mathematics coaches first need to know what challenging and rigorous lessons are *not*. They are not

- more problems for the students to solve,
- problems simply using larger, more complex numbers,
- a faster pace with more skills introduced,
- more independent work, or
- less explanation from the teacher.

Challenging and rigorous problems make students think mathematically. They require students to draw on diverse skills and concepts already learned. They also may require students to work with peers to solve problems cooperatively. This is "purposeful learning," which the National Research Council (NRC; 2001) has characterized as follows: "There is growing evidence that students learn best when they are presented with academically challenging work that focuses on sense making and problem solving as well as skill building" (p. 335). These types of mathematics problems encourage—indeed, require—students to formulate plans and carry them out in order to reach answers, to test the soundness of their answers within the problem situations and constraints, and to justify their thinking and conclusions.

Having an appropriate mathematics curriculum is vitally important to coaches. It strongly affects the process of teaching, the focus of learning, and the reliability of assessment data. The curriculum content document serves as a contour map of the mathematical terrain. If the map is inaccurate or not to scale, then the likelihood of teachers and students getting lost is high.

ALIGNING THE CURRICULUM

All teachers have some form of content document and methods guide, though in some cases these documents may be more in the teachers' heads than on paper. They may, by default, be based on a textbook. And they present themselves in teachers' lesson plans. However, as we indicated in Part I, all too often the "present" in curriculum and instruction as manifested in classrooms is inadequate to the needs of students. Mathematics coaches can change this by helping teachers learn what needs to improve and then helping them do it. Change starts with the curriculum: a content document that is reasonable in length and aligned to state standards. The methods guide is next: one that is inclusive and provides effective instructional strategies that increase student learning for every student.

The following approaches, provided in outline form, are designed to assist mathematics coaches in aligning the adopted curriculum to identified state standards with regard to (1) mathematics content (what students should know), (2) learning expectations (what students should be able to do), and (3) effective instructional strategies (how teachers will teach). They are labeled Method A, Method B, and Method C, with the first section applicable to all three approaches. We have included information about developing both a content document and a methods guide.

An aligned curriculum establishes a basis for providing feedback to teachers, administrators, and students. The alignment process requires teachers to work in collaborative groups. Emerging knowledge about effective instructional techniques and the need to adjust instruction to meet individual students' learning needs means that the curriculum improvement process is never truly finished. Collaborative groups allow for more ideas, coherence across classrooms, and continuity across time.

General Principles for Alignment

These points apply to all three approaches: Method A, Method B, and Method C:

- Study state standards for content and learning expectations and collateral supporting or explanatory documents.
- Study curriculum-related documents from the National Council of Teachers of Mathematics, specifically *Principles and Standards for School Mathematics* (2000) and *Curriculum Focal Points* (2006).
- Study district-developed curriculum documents, guides to their interpretation, and current programs for information about content and learning expectations.
- Identify areas of alignment and misalignment of mathematics content. Misalignment may occur because content is missing or inappropriately placed; is insufficient in depth, quality, or quantity; or for other reasons.
- Analyze lesson designs, including approaches and strategies.

At this point the methods diverge. The what-next decision is a judgment call. If the curriculum is reasonably aligned—say, 80%—then minor adjustments may be all that are needed. In this case the local curriculum has adequately provided for state standards and offers effective instructional strategies for teachers that clearly show what students should know and be able to do. Thus, it is reasonable to follow Method A. However, if the curriculum is deficient or significantly misaligned, then follow Method B or C.

Method A moves the mathematics coach and collaborating teachers toward developing a methods guide. Method B tackles development of an aligned content document first and then moves toward a methods guide. Method C presents an alternative to achieving curriculum alignment.

Method A

To develop a methods guide, the collaborators should do the following:

- determine pacing guidelines for the program,
- analyze grade-level and strand data to determine areas of greatest need, and
- make appropriate adjustments to the depth, quantity, format, and other characteristics for each identified objective.

These points are sufficient to move the collaborative planning forward in the development of a methods guide for the aligned curriculum.

Method B

In the case of a deficient or misaligned curriculum, development of the content document will require the collaborators to

- remove inappropriately placed content objectives from the program, including teacher and student materials;
- review objectives of insufficient depth or quality, and add appropriate content or materials;
- review objectives of insufficient quantity, and add or supplement with appropriate content and materials; and
- review missing objectives, locate appropriate places for new content objectives, and then develop or locate supplementary replacement units or lessons for each objective.

With these changes made, the collaborators can move on to creating a methods guide by doing the following:

- examine lesson designs for student learning expectations;
- review district, grade, and strand data;
- locate areas of greatest need;
- research effective instructional strategies that match student learning needs;
- locate or create replacement units with effective strategies; and
- institute instructional change.

These two steps constitute Method B.

Method C

Following is an alternative method for achieving content alignment. What are mathematics coaches to do when the processes discussed above are not followed or are not completed within a reasonable time?

When inappropriate or misaligned content is taught, students receive a double penalty. They are penalized for the time taken to teach the misaligned content and for the appropriate content missed during the same instructional period. Regardless of any prior alignment work, mathematics educators in both elementary and secondary schools are continually challenged with realignment as new textbooks, resources, and materials are placed in classrooms. Mathematics coaches cannot forget that ignoring alignment while changing instructional materials results in losses for students.

It may be natural to assume that newly purchased or adopted materials are more closely aligned to state standards than earlier materials, but that assumption has little basis in fact. If mathematics coaches are told that new resources are aligned, unless the information comes from a mathematics supervisor or coordinator who has done the alignment, then the coaches cannot assume they are aligned. Students still may be learning the mathematics being taught, but their performance on state assessments will suffer if what they are learning does not relate to what is being assessed (English, 2000).

Some school districts have the resources to realign curriculum documents to newly adopted textbooks and to provide matching curriculum guides to mathematics teachers by following Method A or B. This is an efficient, effective, and desirable condition. Mathematics coaches in these situations will work to ensure fidelity of implementation and clarity of understanding.

In other districts and classrooms, new textbooks will be issued, classes will be assigned, teachers will begin teaching, and coaches will begin coaching with minimal, if any, up-front time allocated to aligning the new resources. This virtually guarantees that a misaligned curriculum will be taught.

Time is the usual impediment. Therefore, mathematics coaches may need to break the alignment process into smaller, more manageable parts and to spread alignment work over time. Method C offers such an alternative process, which can be varied according to the needs of coaches and teachers. This small-scale process can and should be repeated with each new instructional unit throughout the year. It also will be cycled over several years as coaches and teachers refine curriculum alignment.

Although segmented and time-consuming, Method C will yield results much like those obtained using the other approaches. For future reference, this approach also is related to the coplanning method that we describe in Chapter 6. Following are the steps of this approach:

1. As in Methods A and B, coaches gather resource materials, especially released test items from state assessments, the primary teaching resource (in most cases the textbook), and a copy of the state standards.

2. Coaches and teachers select an instructional unit to be taught in coming weeks and decide on the number of days to allot to teaching the concepts and skills in the unit. (Note that coaches must keep in mind the time allocated to this unit within the time available during the semester or school year, allowing consideration of the dates of state assessments.)

3. Coaches lead the process by starting at the end of the unit, by reviewing the summative test. The test defines the learning goal and details what students need to know and be able to do when they have completed the unit. In deciding and developing the lessons for the unit, the collaborators will need to

- incorporate practice test items that match the instructional objectives,
- check the alignment of unit test items and the practice items and realign as necessary,
- ensure that representations (concrete, pictorial, numerical, graphical, verbal/written, symbolic) in the standards are appropriately addressed, and
- balance assessment items to ensure a fair and accurate unit test of required skills and concepts.

4. The collaborators examine expectations for student learning in the textbook or other resources. Most textbooks are not aligned to any particular state standards. Therefore, some of the skills they present must be omitted or taught in a different sequence in order to align with state standards.

These four steps compose a process that can be repeated, over time leading to alignment of the entire curriculum at a basic level. However, other important ideas have not yet been addressed, such as data to inform practice, intervention and remediation strategies, and so forth. The four-step process offers a way to initiate alignment of the written, taught, and tested curricula. This process is easy to begin and can serve to foster a deeper process of alignment. At the very least it can be used as a basis for professional conversations about effective lesson planning.

In summary, curriculum alignment is probably the most straightforward of educational improvement efforts. Yet, misalignment remains a major obstacle to equity and increased student achievement (English, 2000; Marzano, 2003). The cumulative effect of pervasive misalignment is not readily observable day to day, but it shows in large-scale assessments and achievement gaps. Other possible effects of misalignment can be seen in the number of remedial mathematics courses offered, patterns of achievement on state assessments when results are disaggregated by socioeconomic group, and student population disparities in higher-level mathematics courses.

CRITICAL POINTS

Providing students with the opportunity to learn the established curriculum is foundational to ensuring equity. Alignment of the written, taught, and tested curricula is the cornerstone for success in student achievement. To begin the improvement effort, mathematics coaches should be primarily concerned with a viable mathematics curriculum aligned to state standards.

5 Implementing the Curriculum as Designed

When mathematics coaches, supervisors, and teachers have an aligned curriculum content document, or the process of developing one is well under way, then implementation becomes the issue. Without effective implementation, instructional change will not occur. To address this issue, mathematics coaches need to monitor implementation by gathering data that answer two questions:

- Are the content document and methods guide being used as intended?
- Is student achievement increasing?

These data will answer questions, sustain change efforts, and allow mathematics coaches to make informed adjustments to their efforts. Monitoring implementation and collecting data are essential, because change can be uncomfortable, and teachers may be hesitant to alter their instructional approaches without clear indicators of the need to do so—and evidence of the positive results when they do.

PROVIDING PROMPT, ACCURATE FEEDBACK

This brings us to the matter of feedback. Coaches gather data from multiple sources and in various ways. What they discover must be communicated to teachers. Giving feedback is a key responsibility. Providing feedback in ways that are prompt, positive, and useful increases the likelihood that such information will be used and therefore positively affect student learning. When there is evidence of increased learning, then it also is more likely that a change effort can be sustained.

Several sources can answer the questions above, one being observation during classroom visits. In Chapter 8 we detail methods of collecting, analyzing, and using data with the goal of informing teachers' instructional decisions regarding specific lessons. In this chapter we are more focused on global aspects of collecting data that show whether the aligned curriculum is being implemented.

BASICS OF COLLECTING DATA

Mathematics coaches should routinely visit classrooms to stay informed about teachers' instructional preparations and lesson deliveries. This is a basic step, but it must be kept in mind that simply covering the curriculum does not ensure that objectives will be met. Classroom observation is a form of monitoring, but monitoring is different from evaluating. In monitoring, mathematics coaches are looking for links between the aligned curriculum and actual instruction. Is the curriculum being properly implemented? Are the lesson objectives clear? Are students engaged?

Data also are collected through district-level assessments that are used to determine overall student learning and to make informed program adjustments. Large-scale assessments also are one way to identify students who need extra assistance or other forms of instructional intervention. Mathematics coaches usually do not have sole responsibility for large-scale assessments but may be asked to work closely with teachers and administrators in selecting some forms of assessment that yield evidence of improvement in student learning.

Schmoker (1999) believes that a way to ensure successful implementation of the aligned curriculum is to employ regular monitoring and then to make adjustments in how implementation is accomplished based on the monitoring results. In successful schools, according to Spillane et al. (2002), effective implementation also results from proactive use of assessments by school leaders:

> The principal has led the effort to run test score analysis on data provided by the district so that teachers can chart the progress of school-level reforms by subject area and grade level. These leadership strategies have shifted the import of test data within the school's improvement agenda—transforming student outcome data from something the district simply demands to a tool that the school fully expects to use. (p. 738)

Data collection and analysis are more involved than simply reading the test data reports. The involvement of an informed, proactive principal in this process is very important. Mathematics coaches work in harmony with various stakeholders in order to obtain and analyze data needed to effectively monitor progress, and the principal is a key stakeholder.

USING DATA TO INFORM INSTRUCTION

When collected data are not returned in the form of useful feedback, problems arise. Teachers reasonably expect to know why data are being collected and how such information will be used. They may assume that unreturned data are negative and reflect badly on their teaching, which can raise trust issues. Mistrust, once established, is hard to change. Mathematics coaches usually are not evaluators and should not inadvertently be made to seem so by the questionable use of data collection.

Mathematics coaches need to be seen as instructional leaders and as change agents who can assist teachers in improving instruction that, in turn, will improve student learning. It is important for coaches to understand differences between evaluation and support. Evaluation is a process of considering or examining something in order to judge its value, quality, importance, or condition. Evaluation compares things—whether objects or actions—or rates them against established norms. School administrators are required to conduct criteria-based teacher evaluations and often use monitoring as a means to collect evaluative data. Because mathematics coaches also use monitoring to collect data, it is easy to see how confusion might arise.

Establishing a supportive mind-set is important. Both coaches and teachers need to see data collection (classroom monitoring, formal assessments, and other strategies) as a way to understand curricular and instructional issues. The aim is for this understanding, which should be achieved collaboratively, to inform instructional practices. This is the nature of support—active assistance and encouragement.

Some mathematics leaders (department heads, for example) with whom coaches work have authority to evaluate; others do not. Those who do, like school principals, struggle with a dual responsibility of gathering data for both evaluation and support. Teachers may have difficulty distinguishing between the two responsibilities. Mathematics coaches are likely to be more effective if they can avoid being cast in this dual role along with principals, department heads, curriculum supervisors, and others who hold similar positions.

UNDERSTANDING AND PRODUCING BENCHMARK ASSESSMENTS

A *benchmark* is a student performance standard, or the level of student competence in a content area. Benchmark assessments measure group performance against an established standard (or set of standards) at defined points along a path toward meeting the standard. Subsequent assessments use the benchmarks to measure progress toward achievement.

The better the system of collecting, analyzing, and disseminating data, the more useful the data are and the greater their positive effect. One method of data collection is the use of benchmarks and benchmark assessments.

All forms of assessment carry some controversy. On one hand, many see assessments as essential for curing education's ills and instrumental for producing effective instruction, increasing student learning, and closing achievement gaps. On the other hand, there are those who see assessments as raising barriers to improvement by reducing teacher creativity, shrinking the curriculum, and reinforcing the achievement gap. How do mathematics coaches navigate these seemingly shark-infested waters?

First, coaches must be conversant about assessments, types and variations, myths, and truths. One truth is that it is virtually impossible to determine student achievement growth without some form of assessment. Reeves (2004) notes, "Only when accountability, standards, and assessments are fully integrated at the classroom level will we achieve the potential for fairness, equity of opportunity, and improved academic achievement that teaching professionals crave and society demands" (p. 107).

Second, mathematics coaches cannot expect teachers, administrators, or other stakeholders to leap from minimal testing to an integrated assessment system in one move. Several steps are needed to develop and implement a plan for effectively using assessments not to evaluate teachers but to improve teaching. This gradual change rests on teachers and instructional leaders, supported by coaches, understanding

- basic terms and components of assessment;
- frameworks of assessment, starting with a foundation of benchmarks; and
- how to build from the foundation and add to the framework to produce an integrated, accurate, and efficient assessment system.

Third, it should be remembered that data are neither positive nor negative. It is the interpretation of data that can be challenging. Data are difficult enough to use accurately when assessments are clearly understood. But when erroneous interpretations are applied to data, a great deal of harm can result. Coaches, mathematics leaders, and teachers need to know what data indicate and what they do not indicate.

Types of Assessments

Basically, assessments fall into two broad categories: norm referenced and criterion referenced. Norm-referenced assessments are designed to rank a student's achievement when compared to large segments of the population. Statistically, the majority of students will score around the 50th percentile. Typically, when arranged in grade-level terms, these types of assessments contain items above, at, and below grade-level performance standards. Large-scale norm-referenced tests usually are provided by testing companies with years of research data on test items and student performance, and the assessments' validity and reliability are statistically supported.

Criterion-referenced assessments are designed to rate a student's achievement compared to a standard. Ideally, every student could correctly answer every question on a criterion-referenced test based on information that the student had studied. Teacher-made tests are examples of this type of assessment. Textbook tests—for example, chapter tests—usually are criterion-referenced. Many, if not most, criterion-referenced test items are not subjected to scrutiny for validity or reliability.

Assessment Mandates

A framework of mandated assessments was set with the passage of the federal No Child Left Behind (NCLB) legislation. Every state is required to use some form of assessment that measures student performance and progress. These assessments are criterion referenced or partially norm referenced. State frameworks are what mathematics coaches and instructional leaders must use. Mathematics coaches must understand the testing framework for two important reasons—what test data *do* reveal and what they *do not* reveal about student achievement and learning.

No matter how extensive a state's mandated testing program, it is not sufficient for improving teaching and learning. Mathematics coaches and instructional leaders cannot base instructional decisions on data collected only once a year. By the time assessment results return to the district or individual school, it is too late to intervene in the instructional process with effective support. This is not to say that state assessment data are not useful or should not be used. However, it does mean that large-scale, mandated-assessment data need to be supplemented with additional, local achievement data.

Local, supplemental assessments will range from tests with multiple-choice items scored against an answer key to multiday, multistep tests with free-response items scored against a rubric.

Professional Conversations

Feedback on these assessments is important, and mathematics coaches and teachers need to have professional conversations about using locally generated assessment data that, by their less formalized nature, may be more challenging to analyze and interpret. Supportive and reflective conversations might touch on some or all of the following and include all forms of assessment data—state assessments, benchmark assessments, classroom assessment, and observations:

- continuing work to improve curriculum and assessments,
- assisting teachers in finding trends and patterns in data,
- assisting teachers in analyzing student work on assessments,
- identifying successes in instructional strategies and other teacher behaviors,
- planning ways to address students' poor performance on objectives, and
- incorporating unused or underused instructional techniques that may gain good results.

Reflecting on practice might also include questions that teachers should consider, such as the following:

- What did I, the teacher, do?
- What did my students do?
- Which of my actions evoked the greatest positive student response?
- What were the outcomes of these actions?

Developing the Assessment System

Mathematics coaches need to consider the development of a school's assessment system. The preceding sections address only the development of a baseline. Once a basic assessment system is in place, generating data and informing instruction, then additional assessment strategies can be implemented.

Disaggregating data to understand student subgroup performance issues is one further step beyond the basic assessment system. Another is to examine ways to understand more fully students' thinking, which often is best accomplished using assessments that rely on open-ended, or free, responses.

Designing assessments is no easy task. Mathematics coaches need to know about and anticipate some common pitfalls as they work in collaboration with teachers to design local assessments. First, they should recognize that initial attempts at writing effective assessment items will not be perfect. Even "borrowed" test items can be flawed. An item may not accurately test an objective, it might have a strong distracter, or it might be biased.

Second, teachers usually are not experts at testing. The assessment items they create will not necessarily be valid or reliable. An item may not accurately reflect the mathematics objective that the state has identified.

Third, in criterion-referenced tests, each item usually is awarded the same weight, even though items range in degree of difficulty. Therefore, an item analysis of the test will be necessary, and this is a time-consuming, often complex task.

Once a common assessment has been developed and administered, it can be scored and the results analyzed. Students often are given a grade on locally developed assessments, but the grade is not the primary objective. Items of any test should be organized by objectives. Resulting clusters of objective-based items can then be disaggregated to give insights into subcategories, such a performance by minority students. Mathematics coaches should lead by

- assisting teachers in analyzing assessment items;
- supporting professional conversations about assessments;
- helping teachers plan how to work on objectives that students have not yet mastered;
- incorporating new, unused, or underused instructional techniques; and
- charting students' progress toward mastery.

Data Management

With so many parties having access to data, a hazard can lie in how the data are used. Local assessment data collected for the purpose of strengthening teaching and learning should be used only for that purpose, and teachers need to be assured that data are not being collected for this purpose and then used to evaluate them. This assurance needs to be a strong message, and mathematics coaches need to voice this message.

Assessment results measured against benchmarks are used to inform instructional planning, usually looking ahead to the next six- or nine-week period. Which objectives were mastered such that the tested information can now be confidently used to deepen students' understanding in preparation for coming concepts? Which objectives were barely met, indicating a need to review certain topics? And which objectives were not achieved? What intervention strategies can be employed to strengthen students' skills or content knowledge in these areas?

Finally, as an instructional unit unfolds, mathematics coaches need to spend time coteaching various parts of the unit. Coaches should capture those strategies that worked well and reserve those that did not work for further consideration, rethinking, or refinement. A key role in data management is for mathematics coaches to help teachers stay on track. Only in this way will data management be made to serve the goal of improving teaching and learning.

In Chapter 6 we look in greater depth at mathematics coaches' role in coteaching and lesson planning.

CRITICAL POINTS

One of the primary responsibilities of mathematics coaches is to work with teachers to ensure the aligned curriculum is actually taught. To this end they need to understand that providing prompt, accurate feedback is key, whether the feedback is based on classroom observations or data from other sources, including federally mandated, state-mandated, and district- and classroom-level assessments.

6 Planning and Coteaching Lessons

I n Chapter 3 we discussed building rapport with teachers, which is the groundwork necessary for collegial, professional relationships. Such relationships are critical to mathematics coaches' success as agents of change that improves teaching and learning. Trust is necessary for all change initiatives and paves the way for coaches to work directly with teachers to improve their use of instructional strategies. To accomplish this end, coaches engage in planning lessons with teachers and in coteaching some lessons.

Cooperative planning and coteaching seldom are the norm in schools, and so getting into classrooms in a positive, supportive manner could be more challenging for coaches than they might expect. The workplace culture in most schools stresses independence and individuality: one teacher, working behind a closed door with his or her students.

ISOLATION AND ITS EFFECTS

Rarely are teachers going to change their instructional processes by working in isolation. Ignoring the effects of teacher isolation can doom change initiatives. Teacher isolation has long been discussed in the education literature. Kenneth and Barbara Tye predicted a failure of school reform efforts in a January 1984 article citing teacher isolation as the culprit. Williams (2006), using research from McLaughlin and Talbot (1993), "showed that teachers who remained isolated while attempting new strategies became frustrated and discouraged and could not sustain the strategies over time" (p. 89). According to Short and Greer (2002), isolation in the classroom is a huge impediment to enacting change efforts.

Mathematics coaches are in a favorable position to counteract the effects of teacher isolation. Coaches are in classrooms frequently and can serve as catalysts for making teaching practice transparent and stimulating professional conversations in which instructional strategies can be shared, analyzed, compared, and adjusted.

CHALLENGES UNIQUE TO MATHEMATICS COACHES

Unlike attitudes toward student learning in other disciplines, a unique belief exists among many stakeholders about the ability of students to learn mathematics. To better understand this, take reading as an example. Reading teachers expect and the public demands that every child learn to read. Reading educators are hammered by news reports about students not able to read at grade level, and these teachers work tirelessly, believing that (1) reading skills are critical to quality of life and future learning success and (2) regardless of how long it takes, all students can learn. There are similar, commonly held expectations that all students can learn history, science, social studies, and other subjects. Failure to learn in all of these areas is more likely to be attributed to teachers' lack of instructional success or students' lack of effort rather than the absence in students of some mythical history gene or science gene.

In mathematics, by contrast, there is a commonly held belief that some students simply cannot learn mathematics. They lack a math gene; it's a fact of nature—or so some seem to believe. As a consequence, it is not unusual to hear the sentiment expressed—by teachers, parents, and others—that, while regrettable, it really is all right to be deficient in mathematics—especially once students have mastered basic computation and can balance their check books. Suffice it to say, this belief is detrimental to accomplishing change in the teaching and learning of mathematics, and coaches will be challenged to change this belief in order to accomplish their goals.

Another challenge, though one that is not unique to mathematics coaches, is getting a foot in the door. Effective coaching requires full hands-on approaches: face-to-face, side-by-side contact with teachers in classrooms on a continuing basis. But the first step is getting not only into classrooms but also into the school. In many cases mathematics coaches are classroom teachers assigned to the role. There may or may not be mathematics coordinators or supervisors in the district. However, a curriculum director or perhaps a building principal will be charged with general oversight of the mathematics coaches, though she or he may not have a clear idea of the role and responsibilities attached to mathematics coaching.

Couple this issue with the fact that many mathematics coaches are provided only vague or ill-defined job descriptions (for example, "improve mathematics achievement") and the probability of success is reduced. It will be incumbent on mathematics coaches to adopt a leadership posture in order to overcome these challenges. So what should mathematics coaches do?

START WITH PLANNING

Mathematics coaches need to be attuned to the fact that the planned lesson is almost always the presented lesson (Kennedy, 2005). As they plan lessons, teachers form a mental script of the lesson flow. This script is followed during the course of a lesson. Armed with this understanding, coaches can positively affect classroom instruction by affecting teachers' planning. This is a good reason to start with planning when attempting to institute change. Another reason to begin with planning is that working collaboratively to plan lessons is far less threatening to teachers than coaches actually entering their classrooms.

Especially in the first round or two of collaborative planning, coaches need most of all to be effective listeners. One role of coaching is to discover teachers' current knowledge and understanding of instructional strategies. Positive changes begin from this point, building on the teachers' knowledge base that coaches discover. The goal, after all, is not for mathematics coaches to prove how much they know but to assist teachers in learning and using effective instructional strategies. Lessons planned by coaches are not likely to be implemented and, in fact, will undermine true collaboration.

Planning to plan is another important initial coaching strategy. Coaches should schedule planning sessions at the convenience of teachers. They should ensure that times, places, and topics (if possible) are established on theirs and teachers' calendars well ahead of meeting. If groups of teachers routinely plan together, attendance by coaches should not be unexpected. Good communication in this regard is part of building rapport, which we discussed in Chapter 3.

Planning in Reverse

We referred to planning in reverse in Chapter 4. The idea refers to starting with the lesson or unit objectives—what students need to learn—and working backward from the end-of-lesson or end-of-unit assessment to structure how teachers will conduct lessons so that students meet the objectives.

Mathematics coaches and teachers have complementary roles in planning lessons that implement the aligned curriculum, but coaching serves to ensure that issues affecting alignment are understood and addressed. Following are basic steps:

1. Coaches gather resource materials, the curriculum content document, the methods guide, and any other germane materials, such as benchmark assessments, state assessments, and last year's unit test results, and ensure that these documents are available at every planning session.

2. Together coaches and teachers select an instructional unit to be taught for the next several weeks. They review the number of days to be allotted to teaching the included concepts and skills. This information may come directly from the curriculum documents if they include suggested instructional time lines.

3. The planning team turns to the end of the unit and reviews the cumulative test, identifying what students are expected to know and do when they have completed the unit. Coaches and teachers reflect on data from prior assessments, such as benchmarks or last year's unit test results, to determine past patterns of errors, misconceptions, and content not mastered. Such reflection assists with identifying students' anticipated strengths and weaknesses.

4. The planning team reviews textbook contents along with the curriculum documents to ensure that instruction using the textbook will align with the curriculum. A couple of questions are worth asking:

   • How do the textbook authors envision the unit unfolding for students?
   • What skills and concepts are developed? Is skill development progressive? Does new content build on prior knowledge?

The planners will need to consider whether students can be expected to have prerequisite skills and whether scaffolding strategies will be needed to convey content that needs emphasis.

Mathematics understanding follows a definite developmental sequence. If a textbook's sequence does not make sense to coaches and teachers, it probably will not make sense to students either. Developing a flowchart of mathematical concepts or skills can aid analysis, reflection, and subsequent planning. An example of such a flowchart is shown in Figure 6.1.

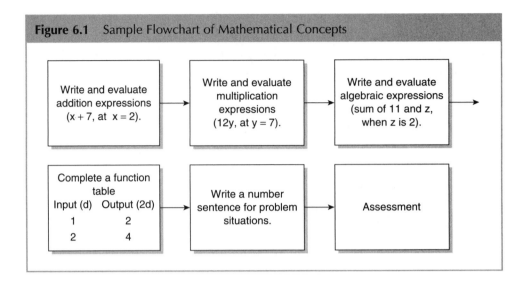

Figure 6.1 Sample Flowchart of Mathematical Concepts

5. Once a plan has been developed, coaches and teachers should carefully reread statements in the resource documents about student learning expectations to ensure that they have a clear understanding of intended outcomes. The plan can then be adjusted, if necessary, to ensure that they have not strayed from the path to the objective during the process of planning. This final step brings the process full circle.

Making the Plan Visible to Students

As instruction begins, teachers should take time to outline the plan of the unit for their students. One way to begin mirrors the start of the planning process: asking students to examine test items they will see at the end of the unit or to examine released or sample test items from aligned large-scale assessments. Teachers might pose the following questions to their students:

- What concepts and skills are you being asked to learn?
- What mathematics vocabulary words are contained in the tests? Which are familiar? Which are new to you?
- What do the directions ask you to be able to do?

After discussing the assessments, teachers may want to ask students to turn to the textbook's table of contents or to page through the unit and highlight important vocabulary, skills, and concepts. Students also need to know how much time is anticipated for each lesson or section of the unit, what the learning goals are for the steps along the way, and a general time line (though teachers will make adjustments as needed to ensure that students reach the objectives).

ENTERING THE CLASSROOM

After a period of successful collaborative planning, it will be time for coaches to schedule times to be in a classroom. They will need to establish in cooperation with teachers how long they will be in the classroom and what they will do there. This information should be incorporated into the unit planning.

What coaches do in classrooms sends messages. The adage that actions speak louder than words was never more true than when coaches are present in classrooms. If a coach stands in the doorway or at the back of a room, sits at a desk, takes notes, or silently walks around a room, then the coach will disrupt the flow of the lesson and send a negative message to the teacher. The coach's presence will signal supervision, rather than observation and assistance. The nonverbal message will trump anything said by coach about why he or she is in the classroom. Clearly spelling out the coach's role in the classroom during unit planning will mitigate this problem.

Coaches also will need to pick their visits carefully. Times when teachers are going to lecture the entire period or administer a test should be avoided. In these cases there is little for a coach to do but observe. Coaches need to participate. For example, coaches might plan to attend part of a teacher's presentation and then work with a small group of students completing an assignment. Coaches also might help teachers answer students' questions or more broadly support students in group work. As much as possible, coaches need to move about a room, assisting students and fitting into the flow of the lesson. Coaches must be seen as providing help, not as posing a psychological threat to classroom teachers.

At the same time coaches should be cautious about settling into any permanent assistive role. If they do, they will find themselves tutoring struggling students or being assigned some other activity on a regular basis. That would diminish their ability to accomplish the real goal of coaching—to improve teaching and learning, to create true change.

As teachers become comfortable with the presence of coaches in the classroom, then coaches can begin to introduce new ideas and new instructional strategies. This is not just a matter of adding a strategy here and there. The integration of alternatives into teachers' traditional instructional approaches begins with the collaboration on unit planning and individual lesson design. It is carried forward as coaches work in classrooms.

Mathematics classrooms that are centers of high-level learning exhibit a particular look and feel. There is energy within the room. Coaches intuitively recognize this energy; they see it in the eyes of students and hear it in the voices of teachers. But it is difficult to communicate intuition. Therefore, it is helpful to have a set of characteristics to which coaches can refer when they engage teachers in professional conversations about the dynamics of highly successful mathematics classrooms. Figure 6.2 provides a list of these characteristics.

Figure 6.2   How Should a Mathematics Classroom Look and Feel?

- Students and teachers have spirit, emotion, enthusiasm, and respect.
- Students and teachers are sharing, discussing, and explaining.
- Students are working independently, with partners, and in groups.
- Classroom work is challenging, engaging, and relevant.
- Various resources are used as appropriate.
- Teachers are using multiple strategies to encourage and engage students.
- Multiple representations of mathematics are used, such as those that are concrete, pictorial, graphical, numerical, and symbolic.
- Opportunities for frequent formative assessments occur for students and teachers to capture and refine thinking.

These characteristics are general guides for mathematics coaches to use in collaborative planning. They emphasize active, engaged student learning. They can be adapted or supplemented as needed, and in most cases teachers will need more detailed information about the characteristics in order to translate them into effective classroom practice.

COTEACHING

When mathematics coaches have become a well-accepted presence in classrooms, teachers will feel more comfortable about the prospect of coteaching. In the context of mathematics coaching, coteaching means that the coach and the teacher will share responsibility for instruction in certain circumstances.

Coteaching is not the same as demonstration teaching, in which the coach might take the place of the teacher as the instructor with the regular teacher taking the role of observer. While demonstration teaching is a form of modeling, it is more intrusive and likely to be less comfortable for teachers. In true coteaching, teachers and coaches first plan collaboratively the roles that each will play. Neither will be the lead teacher or the assistant teacher. A level of equality is maintained.

However, coteaching does offer an opportunity for coaches to introduce and model new instructional strategies or new approaches to traditional techniques. Coaches also ensure that what they do and what teachers do conform to the standards established by the curriculum content document and implement the strategies found in the methods guide.

Once this balanced form of coteaching is well established and teachers are comfortable in their collaborative relationship with coaches, then lessons can be planned with greater flexibility. For example, if a particularly challenging strategy is being introduced, the coach might take on the lead role for that lesson with the teacher acting in a supporting role. Conversely, the teacher might want to try implementing a new strategy with the coach providing support and guidance only if needed.

Many coaches find that coteaching is a natural result of collaborative planning, or coplanning for short. Others have to work harder to make the transition from coplanning to being a presence in the classroom and then to coteaching. Following are some points to remember:

- Coplanning can emerge naturally as a result of professional development activities, adoption of new textbooks or other teaching materials, or the introduction of new strategies or new technology.
- Coaches need to establish specific times to coplan and, when the appropriate level of rapport has been reached, to coteach. Collaboratively establishing a calendar for coplanning and coteaching often is best done during department meetings or professional learning sessions.
- Coteaching provides for the nonthreatening introduction of new instructional strategies.

Coplanning and coteaching serve another important purpose for mathematics coaches. In Chapter 5 we discussed collecting and using data for feedback on alignment. When coaches are working with teachers to coplan lessons, they increase the alignment of the material and the likelihood that a lesson will be delivered as planned. By coteaching they also gain firsthand knowledge of how a lesson was taught, which will inform subsequent professional conversations.

Sharing Instructional Responsibility

As coaches and teachers become comfortable with coteaching, they can trade primary and supporting roles depending on the nature of the lesson. Either the coach or the classroom teacher can serve as the primary teacher. The primary teacher

- decides on learning goals,
- determines the flow of the lesson,
- directs the learning activities, such as initiating exploration activities,
- determines the timing of the lesson components, and
- summarizes the learning.

Even though the primary teacher manages the flow, he or she may not be responsible for conducting every component of the lesson. Some may be conducted by the supporting teacher. In general, the supporting teacher

- follows the pace and flow of the primary teacher,
- supports the work of individual students or small groups,
- conducts one or more of the lesson components,
- monitors activity in the classroom, and
- focuses on students who seem to be having difficulty.

If the support teacher is conducting one of the lesson components, such as exploration, the primary teacher moves about the room to monitor and help students. The primary teacher is responsible for transitioning the exploration component into the summarization one. This flow between roles takes time to work efficiently. Even though a coach and a teacher may feel the transition is awkward, chances are the students will not even notice.

One caveat must be stated, however. Even when sharing responsibility, the ultimate responsibility for classroom instruction rests with the teacher, not the coach. Coaches are, in practical terms, guests; it is classroom teachers who must deal with students when coaches are not present.

BEING A VALUABLE RESOURCE

To be a valuable resource during planning and coteaching, mathematics coaches must know state standards, state and district assessments, district curriculum content documents and methods guides, and the textbooks and other instructional materials. Taken together, these provide instructional guidance that is aligned in order to improve teaching and learning. A fundamental goal of mathematics coaching is to ensure that all mathematics teachers are teaching the aligned curriculum. Coaches cannot help plan lessons that are aligned if they do not know the mathematics standards, nor can coaches help plan or teach lessons that prepare students for mastery if they do not know what and how students will be assessed. All components need to work together, and the mathematics coaches need to ensure that this happens.

But mathematics coaches also must be repositories of effective instructional strategies. These strategies are essential in planning and coteaching. And they need to be carefully chosen, because too many strategies in a lesson can be as ineffective as too few. In this chapter we outline some of the strategies that mathematics coaches must ensure are in their repertoires.

EMPHASIS ON INCLUSIVENESS

Effective teaching requires a wealth of readily available instructional strategies, both general and specific. Teachers need to be able to move fluidly from general strategies to targeted ones. The strategies included in this chapter are effective and inclusive—that is, they invite all students into learning. Inclusiveness is particularly important, because students are heterogeneous in almost all classrooms. For example, in classrooms with one or more English-language learners (ELL), teachers need to be well versed in a variety of instructional strategies that meet the learning needs not only of native speakers of English but also of students who may be struggling to learn English. The same can be said of students with disabilities or learning challenges, such as attention deficit disorder.

In a study conducted by the National Research Council (NRC, 2005) on how students learn, the following fundamental principles of learning were identified for teaching meaningful mathematics:

1. Students come to the classroom with preconceptions about how the world works. If their initial understanding is not engaged, they may fail to grasp the new concepts and information, or they may learn them for purposes of a test but revert to their preconceptions outside the classroom.

2. To develop competence in an area of inquiry, students must (a) have a deep foundation of factual knowledge, (b) understand facts and ideas in the context of a conceptual framework, and (c) organize knowledge in ways that facilitate retrieval and application.

3. A metacognitive approach to instruction can help students learn to take control of their own learning by defining learning goals and monitoring their progress in achieving them. (pp. 1–2)

We would emphasize two points from this research. First, meaningful mathematics instruction uses strategies reflective of these principles of learning. Second, in more and more cases, strategies must be used that help students overcome language barriers.

To address these points successfully, teachers also must overcome another challenge, which is organizing instructional strategies so they can be used purposefully. Marzano, Pickering, and Pollock, in *Classroom Instruction That Works* (2001), provide a list of instructional strategies that have been shown to be effective:

- identifying similarities and differences,
- summarizing and note taking,
- reinforcing effort and providing recognition,
- homework and practice,
- nonlinguistic representations,
- cooperative learning,
- setting goals and providing feedback,
- generating and testing hypotheses, and
- cues, questions, and advance organizers. (p. 7)

This list is useful and informative, but teachers cannot simply start at the top and work their way down, one strategy per lesson. Nor can they use the same strategy or set of strategies for every lesson. That would be simplistic and wrong. Teachers must choose strategies that (1) address mathematics principles of learning applicable to the lesson in question and (2) are responsive to the characteristics and needs of their students.

Reys and colleagues (2007) offer another set of guiding principles that can help teachers make decisions about instructional strategies:

Principle 1: Students should be actively involved in learning mathematics.

Principle 2: Mathematics learning is a developmental process.

Principle 3: Mathematics learning should build on previous learnings.

Principle 4: Communication is an integral part of mathematics learning.

Principle 5: Good and interesting questions facilitate mathematics learning.

Principle 6: Multi-embodiment aids in learning mathematics.

Principle 7: Metacognition affects mathematics learning.

Principle 8: Teachers' attitudes influence mathematics learning.

Principle 9: Mathematics anxiety is influenced by how mathematics is learned.

Principle 10: Forgetting is a natural aspect of learning, but retention can be aided. (p. 22)

Ideally, an instructional sequence and complementary strategies will aim to teach all students the targeted mathematics content to 100% mastery within the shortest reasonable time. Classrooms are rarely ideal, but this is the goal of effective instruction—and the one that coaches strive to help teachers and students meet. Teachers who employ only one dominant strategy, no matter how effective it is in the ideal, will find that it is not effective in the reality of a diverse classroom. One lesson approach cannot possibly be successful for every student. Also, teachers cannot include every possible strategy in every lesson. Mathematics coaches support teachers through planning and coteaching to understand and correctly use strategies that match the objectives of knowledge and skill acquisition and the learning needs of the students in a given class.

GENERAL APPROACHES

Two general approaches emerge from research that may serve as launch points for other, more specific strategies:

- encouraging student collaboration in the form of teamwork (Marzano et al., 2001; Starnes, 2006; Wagner, 2005) and
- using "group-worthy" problems (Boaler, 2006).

These approaches are particularly helpful to ELL students because they provide multiple opportunities to incorporate specific strategies that will assist *all* students. Group-worthy problems enable student collaboration and encourage students to use many approaches to learning, such as generating and testing hypotheses, taking notes and summarizing, tackling hands-on experiences with the teacher as facilitator, and engaging in high-level dialogue and meaning-making (Marzano et al., 2001; Starnes, 2006).

Marzano et al. (2001) note that if students are allowed to show their work and explain their thinking, then sharing information among peers reinforces effort and provides recognition. Sharing also can encourage students to develop visual representations of concepts, which particularly aids learning for students who are language challenged. Effective functioning of student groups also requires teachers to master the arts of questioning and providing prompts and cues. Students need a purpose for working in groups, and this purpose is met by challenging tasks. Challenges can be increased or decreased for individual group needs by teachers asking questions or providing prompts. Encouraging student collaboration and using group-worthy problems are research-based approaches and generally are effective for all students.

Another aspect of student collaboration is peer tutoring (Wagner, 2005). This form of one-on-one collaboration also increases student dialogue. For example, students can check their understanding of a mathematics concept or skill by working with a partner. Classmates help one another catch mistakes and correct misunderstandings. Peer tutoring can be used in conjunction with any of the specific strategies described in the next section.

SPECIFIC STRATEGIES

Although the approaches above are highly recommended and provide many opportunities to incorporate specific strategies, they are not required for effective instruction. In many cases, teachers do not have access to group-worthy problems or may be uncomfortable with collaborative learning groups, at least for certain lessons. The key is for teachers to be attuned to students' thinking and thus able to identify both what students understand and what they do not yet grasp. Effective teaching employs strategies that build on students' understandings and confront their misconceptions (NRC, 2000). It is important to make students' thinking visible, often through dialogue: teacher–student and student–student. Following are a few recommended strategies that should be in mathematics coaches' repertoires and that teachers can use with or without grouping.

Vocabulary

Preteaching vocabulary provides an important opportunity to stress fundamentals before exploring lesson or unit content in depth. Taking time to discuss words—drawing attention to similar words; pointing out important roots, prefixes, suffixes, even letters—helps students learn the definitions of terms they will encounter in the coming lesson or unit. It sets the stage for knowledge acquisition. Many terms are important to mathematical understandings and processes For example, *mean, median, average, sine,* and *square* are used in particular ways in mathematics, though some of these words may be used differently in everyday conversation. Learning vocabulary up front will assist with reading fluency and increase students' reading comprehension.

Visuals and Manipulatives

Models, pictorial representations, graphic organizers, and flow charts that show whole-to-part relationships help students make associations that are important for knowledge acquisition. Visuals help many students make sense of and organize ideas. Often visuals also can be created, adapted, rearranged, and otherwise manipulated to increase learning. For example, students may understand concepts more readily if they are able to manipulate tiles or cubes to represent a problem and its solution(s). Graphic organizers help students identify critical elements and terms and the relationships among them. Displays, diagrams, and charts simplify information and help students see patterns. Before starting an instructional unit, teachers should consider providing students with an overview using pictures, charts, or diagrams or allowing students to construct organizers around their current knowledge (Jensen, 1998; Starnes, 2006).

Technological Aids

Related to models and pictorial representations in many ways is the use of technological aids to learning and processing information. For example, calculators can allow students to test hypotheses and to see patterns. Computer programs and graphing calculators can demonstrate graphic images of mathematical processes. In Figure 6.3, for instance, computer graphs show a variety of transformations of a base function $y = x^2$.

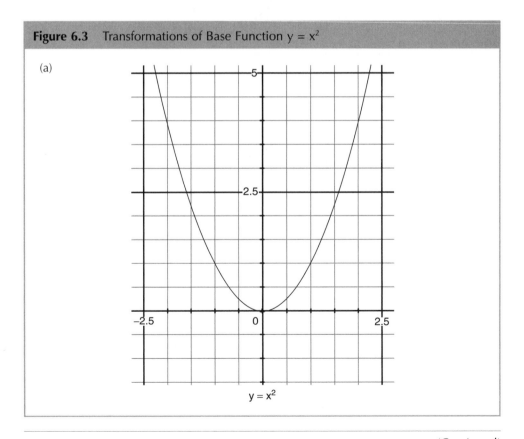

Figure 6.3   Transformations of Base Function $y = x^2$

(a)

$y = x^2$

(Continued)

Figure 6.3 (Continued)

(b)

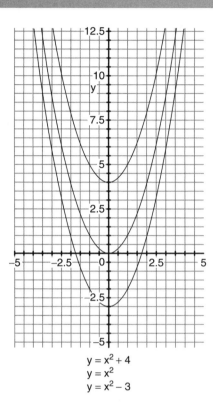

$$y = x^2 + 4$$
$$y = x^2$$
$$y = x^2 - 3$$

(c)

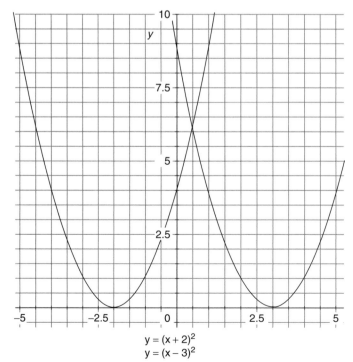

$$y = (x + 2)^2$$
$$y = (x - 3)^2$$

(d)

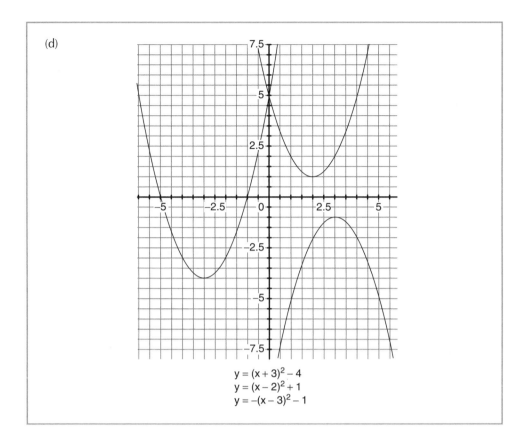

$$y = (x + 3)^2 - 4$$
$$y = (x - 2)^2 + 1$$
$$y = -(x - 3)^2 - 1$$

Scaffolding

Instructional scaffolding refers to providing supports that promote learning when concepts and skills are first introduced. These supports may include templates, guides, or other resources that facilitate the development of content understanding and process skills. Scaffolding strategies introduce students to important prerequisite concepts and skills prior to immersion into new material. If there is an identified prerequisite skill or concept students must know, it is worth the time for teachers to structure activities around these skills prior to introducing new material.

In conclusion, student passivity is no longer the prevailing ethos in most successful classrooms. Humans are social beings, and language is a vital learning tool (NRC, 2000). Teachers meet growing demands for improved academic performance by students by finding ways to engage students in active learning while teaching the aligned curriculum and maintaining an orderly, though not necessarily silent, classroom. Lessons that are built on using the approaches and strategies we have outlined make thinking visible—both teachers' plans for instruction and students' grasp of important content and skills. They also address various learning styles and, in many cases, language challenges.

An overarching concept that applies to all of this is *transfer*. Transfer is a learning phenomenon critical for teachers to understand. It is not an approach or a strategy per se. Transfer has to do with the connecting of ideas. Positive transfer increases and enhances knowledge; negative transfer creates or reinforces misconceptions. Students (and adults) form mental connective networks to understand and retrieve, or recall, information. They seek attributes that seem to make sense and are based on their current level of understanding and then mentally file the information accordingly. An example of negative transfer is evidenced when students routinely confuse the terms and computations for *mean*, *median*, and *mode*. The words all start with the letter *m* and usually are taught within the same lesson or unit. They are statistical measures calculated on the same set of numbers. Without special emphasis over time and ample opportunities for students to discuss how these measures are similar and different, students may confuse them through negative transfer (NRC, 2000). Appropriate discussion and practice, however, will result in positive transfer; students will know and routinely use these measures correctly.

Mathematics coaches can help to ensure that teachers master the approaches and strategies discussed in this chapter by using the same approaches and strategies to enhance their work with teachers during collaborative planning and coteaching.

CRITICAL POINTS

Mathematics coaches achieve success as change agents by building collegial relationships with teachers. Collaborative planning, or coplanning, is a starting point. From there coaches can move into becoming a presence in the classroom. Coteaching can be used to help teachers integrate effective group-oriented and individualized approaches and strategies into their teaching and improve their practice.

7 Making Student Thinking Visible

The mathematics coach's work is based on a foundation of research on effective classrooms, effective instructional strategies, and characteristics of effective teachers. Indeed the topics and references that follow may be used as a reading list for current and prospective coaches:

- Alignment, opportunity to learn, implementation (English, 2000; Marzano, 2003; National Research Council [NRC], 2004b; Williams, 1996).
- Connections to learning, addressing preexisting understandings (Loucks-Horsley et al., 2003; National Council of Teachers of Mathematics [NCTM], 2000; NRC, 1999, 2000, 2002, 2005).
- Thinking about thinking (metacognition), making thinking visible, feedback (NRC, 1999, 2000).
- Sense making, self-assessment, and reflection; transfer of knowledge related to degree of understanding (NRC, 1999, 2002, 2004a, 2005).
- Variety of strategies; grouping, community of learners (Boaler, 2006; Jensen, 1998; Marzano, 2003; NRC, 2002, 2004a; Reeves, 2006).
- Time to learn (Marzano, 2003; NCTM, 2000; NRC, 1999).
- Academically challenging work, active participation, student engagement (NRC, 2001, 2002, 2004a, 2005; Stronge, 2007).
- Teacher expectations (NRC, 2001, 2004a; Reeves, 2006; Stronge, 2007).
- Effort over innate talent (Dweck, 2006; NRC, 2002).

These topics are important considerations for teachers when planning lessons, but effectively infusing these characteristics into the classroom can be complicated. A unifying device will help, and one that is research based is *making students' thinking visible*. The NRC (2000) puts it this way:

"Students' thinking must be made visible (through discussions, papers, or tests), and feedback must be provided. Given the goal of learning with understanding, assessments and feedback must focus on understanding, and not only on memory for procedures or facts" (p. 128). A point of support worth noting, also from NRC (2000), is this: "The roles of assessment must be expanded beyond the traditional concept of testing. The use of frequent formative assessment helps *make student's thinking visible to themselves, their peers, and their teacher* (p. 19, italics added). Too often teachers assume that students are thinking in particular ways. But clear, productive thinking, much like curriculum alignment, does not just happen and cannot be assumed.

CHARACTERISTICS OF VISIBLE THINKING

Why should teachers work to make students' thinking visible? Following are characteristics to note. Visible thinking

- provides clear evidence of student understanding;
- facilitates ongoing monitoring;
- alerts teachers to errors, misconceptions, or incomplete concepts;
- improves teachers' ability to scaffold;
- allows students to self-monitor and self-reflect;
- allows students opportunities to clarify thoughts and reject or affirm ideas;
- allows for immediate feedback;
- allows teachers time to make adjustments in instruction;
- provides greater opportunity to link prior learning;
- increases student participation and engagement;
- increases attention to important concepts;
- increases retention of learning;
- reduces the need to reteach; and
- invites students to become active participants in the learning process.

These characteristics come with a set of prerequisites for teachers. In order to help students to think about their thinking and to gain the teaching and learning benefits of visible thinking, teachers must

- understand mathematical concepts, elements, and connections;
- understand common misconceptions and errors;
- listen carefully and completely to students; and
- make appropriate adjustments to their teaching based on how and what students think.

Figure 7.1 provides an example of how a problem might be approached consistent with these two lists of characteristics.

Figure 7.1 Sample Approach to Visible Thinking: Properties of Numbers

As students progress through a K–12 mathematics curriculum, they encounter a variety of numbers and operations on these numbers. Properties are added along the way to create mathematical systems that have particular structures, some similar and some different. For example, the Natural Numbers under addition have no additive identity, whereas the Whole Numbers under addition do have an additive identity. Not until they take Algebra II in high school, or possibly Algebra I, will students work with Complex Numbers. The point to be made using the Euler diagram below, where examples of numbers in each set are shown, is that students and teachers need to see the big picture of mathematics; however, mathematics coaches may need to provide that picture.

Starting in the elementary grades, students solve simple equations such as $n + 3 = 5$. The solution, $n = 2$, is initially a Natural or Whole Number. Before long, equations such as $n + 5 = 2$ are introduced, where the solution, $n = -3$, is a negative Integer. Soon equations are introduced where the solution is a fraction (Rational Number), such as $4n + 3 = 2$, where $n = -1/4$. Late in Algebra I, or certainly in Algebra II, students solve quadratic equations, where solutions sometimes come from the Irrational Numbers, such as $x^2 + 1 = 3$, where $x = \pm \sqrt{2}$, and then equations such as $x^2 = -4$, where $x = \pm 2i$, and x is a Complex Number.

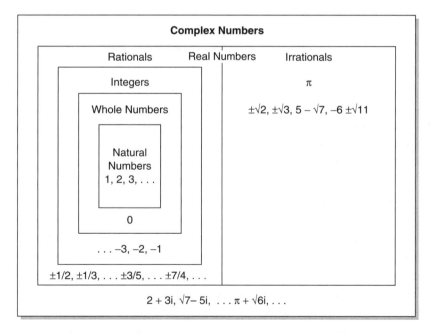

By fifth or sixth grade, students have used numbers from several number systems. Around this time in their learning, students should become familiar with the idea that additional systems exist and will be introduced in the coming years.

HOW THE TRADITIONAL MODEL FALLS SHORT

If we take as given that students need lessons and instructional strategies that invite them to make thinking visible, then how might mathematics coaches use available resources to support and encourage effective teaching? We have mentioned a number of resources and strategies in this and previous chapters. Another resource should be added—namely, *PRompt Intervention in Mathematics Education*, or PRIME (Wagner, 2005), developed by the Ohio Resource Center for Mathematics, Science, and Reading following a conference by that title. The following strategies are included in PRIME:

- learning centers,
- cooperative learning,
- peer tutoring,
- visualization with physical models,
- visualization with drawing,
- building on students' informal knowledge, and
- making connections through reflection.

Previously we listed the following strategies identified by Marzano, Pickering, and Pollock (2001). These strategies work well with the PRIME strategies, which are

- identifying similarities and differences,
- summarizing and taking notes,
- reinforcing effort and providing recognition,
- homework and practice,
- nonlinguistic representations,
- cooperative learning,
- setting goals and providing feedback,
- generating and testing hypotheses, and
- cues, questions, and advance organizers.

Careful readers will note that both lists of strategies include actions by teachers, students, or both. For mathematics coaches it will be important to examine these strategies in the context of a traditional teaching model.

Using this traditional teaching model (cited in the 2000 document, *Before It's Too Late: A Report to the Nation from The National Commission on Mathematics and Science Teaching for the 21st Century*, and identified by the Trends in International Mathematics and Science Study, or TIMSS), teachers routinely continue a lesson from the previous day as if there had been no lapse of time between one lesson and the next. Additionally, in this model, teachers conduct classroom discussions using a process identified by the NRC (2001) as "recitation," in which teachers ask students a series of low-level, short-answer questions. The *Before It's Too Late* report calls this traditional model "numbingly predictable" (p. 20) and describes it as consisting of six steps:

1. a review of previous material and homework,

2. a problem illustration by the teacher,

3. drill on low-level procedures that imitate those demonstrated by the teacher,

4. supervised seat work by students, often in isolation,

5. checking of seat work problems, and

6. assignment of homework. (p. 20)

Where in this model would teachers use or apply the effective instructional strategies listed by Marzano and colleagues (2001) or PRIME, and what would teachers and students be doing? Mathematics coaches can readily see that most of the strategies do not fit within the traditional model. Peer tutoring could be used to assist students with procedural knowledge. And as a reinforcing effort, providing recognition, homework, and practice can be used. But the other recommended strategies are difficult to employ in this model of instruction, which pervades mathematics classrooms.

Of course, a teacher using a recitation approach might use praise to reinforce effort and provide recognition, and homework is already included. But the matter of homework also bears examination. Education researchers commonly stress two purposes. First, homework can be used to add additional practice of a skill. Second, homework also may be used as a way to set the stage for learning or to elaborate or extend learning that has occurred. In working with students and successfully using homework as a learning tool, it is important for teachers to identify the purposes of homework. The recitation approach seems to address only the first purpose.

PRIME also discusses peer tutoring. This is an intervention strategy to help students who may be struggling with a particular skill or concept. Classmates who are more proficient with the skill can help struggling peers. Peer tutoring also can be more formalized and more broadly applied, for example, when older students tutor younger ones. In either case, peer tutoring is more than just getting students to complete an assignment.

Incorporating effective instructional strategies into the traditional model is difficult and with some strategies impossible. It is easy to see that the model does not make students' thinking visible. In fact, it obscures students' thinking. Furthermore, it hides teachers' thinking from students.

CONSTRUCTING AN ALTERNATIVE TO THE TRADITIONAL MODEL

In order to incorporate newer, more inclusive instructional strategies, mathematics coaches need to help teachers rethink and revise the current recitation model. Teachers need a familiar framework but one that is more open and flexible. One suggestion is a lesson format that uses three steps: (1) setting the stage, (2) exploration, and (3) summarization.

This alternative format allows for the use of multiple strategies from various sources. Teachers can select strategies to use in each step. For example, "setting the stage" is a time for teachers to provide scaffolding information and to engage students' interest. "Exploration" is a time for students to work with problems using a variety of perspectives, including prior knowledge. It is an ideal time for cooperative learning so that students can discuss their ideas with their classmates. Finally, "summarization" is an opportunity for teachers to check for student understanding of important concepts in the lesson and to assess accuracy and proficiency of skills.

This model is not designed to fit into a single instructional day, although it might. The model can be used flexibly to span several days of instruction. Often, especially with complex concepts and processes, students need extended time to comprehend new concepts and build new skills. Thus a multiday approach may be preferred. Whether the time span is short or long, it accommodates the type of unit planning we have discussed in previous chapters.

Later in this chapter we will present two sample lessons. In preparation, however, it will be helpful to summarize strategies from Marzano et al. (2001) and PRIME (Wagner, 2005) matched to the three steps of the alternative model.

Setting the Stage

Marzano and colleagues suggest

- identifying similarities and differences,
- reinforcing effort and providing recognition,
- nonlinguistic representation,
- setting goals and providing feedback, and
- generating and testing hypotheses.

PRIME suggests

- visualization with physical models,
- visualization with drawing,
- building on student informal knowledge, and
- making connections through reflection.

Exploration

Marzano and colleagues suggest:

- identifying similarities and differences,
- summarizing and note taking,
- reinforcing effort and providing recognition,
- nonlinguistic representations,
- cooperative learning,
- generating and testing hypotheses, and
- cues, questions, and advance organizers.

PRIME suggests

- learning centers,
- cooperative learning,
- peer tutoring,
- visualization with physical models,
- visualization with drawing,
- building on student informal knowledge, and
- making connections through reflection.

Summarization

Marzano and colleagues suggest:

- identifying similarities and differences,
- summarizing and note taking,
- reinforcing effort and providing recognition,
- homework and practice,
- nonlinguistic representations,
- generating and testing hypotheses, and
- cues, questions, and advance organizers.

PRIME suggests

- visualization with physical models,
- visualization with drawing,
- building on student informal knowledge, and
- making connections through reflection.

Using this instructional model increases possibilities for numerous appropriate strategies to be used. It also allows for students to be "doing" mathematics in a challenging way that causes them to think and to work with other students who are thinking. Thus, teachers can better observe, question, and listen to students to make visible students' and their own thinking. Mathematics coaches and teachers also benefit from the use of this model, because it informs their professional conversations about planning.

Following are two sample lessons that demonstrate the flexibility of this model. The first concerns a problem typical of an Algebra I or Geometry class. The second problem would usually be found in an elementary mathematics class. After each lesson we include a section that discusses collaborative learning opportunities in the lesson.

Sample Lesson 1: Exploring *Pi*

Setting the Stage

The teacher might say, "During your time in mathematics classes, you have studied various aspects of a circle. What terms do you remember that refer to a circle?" As students respond, the teacher lists the terms on the board or chart paper. The teacher then might say, "One special relationship is described by a value named *pi*. That's the relationship we will explore in this lesson."

Exploration

Pairs or small groups of students will need a length of string, a meter stick or metric ruler, and numerous circular items, such as coffee can lids. The more types, sizes, and varieties of circular lids or objects, the better. The teacher might ask students to begin bringing in lids several days prior to the lesson. During the lesson students can share the lids by measuring them and then passing them on to another group.

On the day of the lesson, the groups are given the circular objects and an activity handout partially illustrated below:

Item	Circumference (c)	Diameter (d)	Ratio (c/d)	Decimal Form (c ÷ d)

The teacher asks the students to fill in the first four columns for their objects. They use the string to wrap around the object and then measure the length of the string. They then measure the diameter of the object and record that. After the students have measured their objects, they record the ratio (c/d) and then divide to find the decimal form, which they list in the fifth column. They can use a calculator for the division computation.

Summarization

The teacher might ask students to share findings across groups or ask them to average their answers and write them on the board or display them using an overhead projector. Discussions follow about what can be generalized from the formula $c = \pi d$. These discussions also include what the graph would look like for domain d and range c. The teacher might ask, "Is it reasonable to assume that the diameter of a circle would directly relate to the circumference?"

Collaboration in Action

During the exploration phase of the lesson, students work as partners or in small groups. Typically one student holds the object while another wraps the string around it, and then perhaps a third student measures the string. One of the students records the measurements. The division of labor is unimportant. What matters is that effective collaboration actively involves all of the students.

Sample Lesson 2: Finding Equivalent Fractions

Setting the Stage

The teacher takes a sheet of unlined paper and asks students to describe it. After listening to their responses the teacher folds the paper in half, making two sections, and asks the students to describe it again. The teacher asks, "Can I label the sections?" Then the teacher folds the paper again so that it has four sections and asks, "What can you tell me about the paper now? Can I label the sections? What do you notice about the section I labeled one-half earlier? Does it have another name? (two-fourths). One-half and two-fourths are equivalent fractions. Why do you think mathematicians named them *equivalent?*"

Exploration

Initially, teachers may want younger students or students with little experience in collaboration to work in pairs, instead of in small groups. Eventually, however, teachers will want to structure groups of three or four students so that the students can practice collaboration skills.

Each pair or group should be given four strips of paper of equal length. The teacher will ask, "What do you notice about these strips?" As the students work, the teacher leads them to label one strip "1"; another strip is folded in half, and the halves are each labeled "1/2." The next strip is folded in half and then in half again, making four sections to be labeled "1/4." The procedure is repeated with an additional fold in the fourth strip, and the resulting sections are labeled "1/8."

The teacher and the students then discuss the equivalent fractions, writing the various equivalents on the board. The students may be given the tasks of (1) finding and recording as many equivalent fractions as they can and then (2) organizing their findings in some form of chart.

Summarization

In wrapping up this lesson, the teacher might ask students to discuss their findings. Questions might include the following: What did you discover about the strip labeled "1"? What is true about the numerator and the denominator? Are there other fractions besides the ones we used? Can you name some of them? What do you notice about the relationship between numerators and denominators? What are the critical aspects of equivalent fractions?

Collaboration in Action

In the exploration phase, students work together to manipulate and label the fraction strips. Each student is responsible for one or more strips, but the whole group is watching to ensure accuracy in folding and measuring. After the strips are labeled, the students compare their strips to find equivalent fractions.

In an effective group, students quickly realize that they must agree on an organizational method. Keys to effective collaboration in this lesson include

- sharing ideas,
- recording findings in a common group chart,
- sharing the fraction strips, and
- allowing each member of the group to find an equivalent pair.

By observing students' tone of voice and body language, the teacher can identify whether a group is working collaboratively and guide groups that are experiencing problems.

EFFECTING CHANGE OVER TIME

Coaches can have a positive effect on instruction by helping teachers plan and implement lessons such as these using the suggested alternative model. This model encourages teachers to reflect on their teaching and students to reflect on their learning. The recitation model offers little reason or opportunity for true reflection. In that model the students are passive and so their thinking is not visible.

In the alternative model, students are actively "doing"—and that leads to analysis and reflection that teachers can observe. Thus, teachers also engage in reflection about how the strategies they use affect students' learning. Which activities or techniques increased students' interest and engagement? Where in a lesson did students really seem to "get it," and where did they seem to flounder? When teaching this lesson again, what needs to be repeated and what needs to be done differently?

Mathematics coaches help teachers engage in active reflection as they review and analyze lessons presented and plan for future lessons. The steps that coaches can suggest are straightforward: plan, present, analyze, reflect, and adjust. These steps can produce both short-term improvements and long-term gains. In the short term, coaches ask questions such as the following:

- What do we do next week?
- Where did students struggle or have misunderstandings?
- What can we do to address these needs?

For long-term improvements, the questions include these:

- What did we do last year?
- What were the results?
- Where do students usually have difficulties?
- What do we need to do to address these issues?

GROUP PLANNING

Just as students benefit from peer learning in collaborative groups, so too can teachers benefit from group planning beyond the coplanning that mathematics coaches and teachers do together one on one. Coaches can be instrumental in helping teachers develop collaborative groups for lesson and unit planning.

Coaches usually have little, if any, input in the teaching schedule. But many schools schedule so that various teachers have common planning periods. In these instances the opportunity for group planning is available, and coaches can help teachers take advantage of it. This will require support not only from the teachers but also from principals and department heads. With this support, coaches can begin to work with teachers to plan in collaborative groups.

In most cases the coach will need to act, first, as an observer, allowing a lead teacher or department head to organize the group to address an issue of current importance. A good approach is for coaches to build rapport with department heads or lead teachers and ask how they, the coaches, can assist them. Often common issues arise when new materials are adopted or when significant student failure rates are noticed. In both such cases the moment may be right to introduce changes in curriculum, to review and adjust curriculum alignment, or to suggest new instructional approaches. Teachers' collaboration in planning can subsequently inform coplanning and coteaching by mathematics coaches and individual teachers.

OBSERVATION AND DEMONSTRATION TEACHING

Two additional strategies are related to the preceding: observation and demonstration teaching. We recommend these strategies to support improvement once the change process has been successfully initiated.

Observation

The idea of observing teachers and students is broad. Observation is valuable for many purposes. In this instance the type of observation we are concerned with is focused on teachers and their use of the alternative model outlined in this chapter.

Teachers want feedback on their teaching from sources they can trust and find credible. Once teachers have recognized the value of the improvement process, they will want to stretch—to see how much they can improve how they teach and to learn additional strategies. One of the best ways to accommodate this is to have an individual observe teachers while they are teaching with the express purpose of critiquing specific strategies. Mathematics coaches can make these types of observations, but the observations also can be done by other teachers who have mastered the strategies in question. Coaches can facilitate the process either by observing or by freeing master teachers to do the observations.

Demonstration Teaching

Demonstration lessons are valuable but not in early stages of coaching for several reasons. First, demonstration teaching tends to send a message to teachers that coaches are "the experts" and by implication teachers are not. This impression does not help build rapport. Second, demonstration teaching sends a message to teachers that what they are doing is wrong and needs to be corrected. Again, whether true or not, this impression interferes with building rapport. Third, demonstration lessons may be too complex to be useful early in the change process. They may contain too much that is new or unfamiliar in terms of changing materials, strategies, and classroom organization. Finally, demonstration lessons can sabotage the change process. If the lesson goes well, it is too easy for teachers to say, "Of course it works for you; you're the expert," "My kids always behave well for strangers, but try teaching them for a week or more," or "That was a great lesson, but I don't have time to plan like that every day." On the other hand, if the lesson goes badly, teachers may say, "What do they expect me to do when the expert can't even teach them?" or "My old strategies work a lot better than those."

When teachers and coaches have established rapport and reached a level of comfort, and when coaches are taking an active role in planning and coteaching, the time may be right for demonstration teaching. Mathematics coaches must be willing to take the risk of trying new strategies—and to switch from being the observer to being observed.

Another form of demonstration teaching can work in teachers' collaborative planning. For example, the first time a student assessment is to be analyzed by the teachers' planning group would be an opportune moment for demonstration teaching. Teachers may be unwilling to risk being embarrassed by poor student performance in front of their peers.

Coaches can demonstrate how to conduct the analysis, leading by example.

In this chapter we have tried to cover a number of topics, all of which have a bearing on the goal of making students' thinking visible. As coaches and teachers work to make students' thinking visible, there is a parallel process going on—namely, making coaches' and teachers' thinking visible for the sake of improving teaching and learning. The process of change is never quick or easy. Coaches will need to feel their way when deciding about teachers' readiness to try new techniques and approaches. According to Hall and Hord (2001), change is a combination of pressure and support. Mathematics coaches cannot exert too much pressure or teachers will resist. Yet, if there is no pressure to change, then change will not happen.

CRITICAL POINTS

To transform classrooms and to move away from a traditional model of teaching that is increasingly ineffective for many students, mathematics coaches must work with teachers in planning and delivering lessons that make students' thinking visible. This will require an alternative model that incorporates collaboration—both among students and among teachers.

8 Analyzing and Reflecting on Lessons

In previous chapters we have mentioned analysis and reflection as essential activities for improving teaching and learning. Helping teachers plan and present lessons gives mathematics coaches background information about what teachers know and do and about how students are responding and learning. This is important, because what coaches do on the basis of this information helps to ensure the curriculum coherence vital to student success. Coherence between lesson design and lesson delivery ensures that students are taught the appropriate content.

Teaching lessons as they are planned is important to accurate analysis in addition to student learning, because data about results are of little value in analysis and reflection if the presented lesson is significantly different from the planned lesson. Carrying out the planned lesson using the strategies included in the plan gives teachers and coaches results that can be analyzed to determine how the strategies worked. Subsequent reflection can then inform decisions about whether those strategies or others should be used in future lessons.

Although mathematics coaches are engaged in collaborating with teachers on planning and teaching some lessons, knowledge of what was planned or how a lesson was delivered is not in and of itself sufficient to plan for instructional improvement. Even if it were, it is impossible for coaches to be present during all of the lessons delivered by teachers. And if coaches are coteaching lessons, they are too involved to be accurate observers. Thus, it is important for coaches to help provide teachers with opportunities to reflect on their lesson delivery and outcomes.

REFLECTION

Before we look at the process of analysis and reflection, it will be helpful to explain what we mean by reflection. The idea of reflection is well established in the professional literature. In brief, reflection is a strategic tool that teachers use to improve teaching and learning. Using this tool effectively requires preparation, training, and organization as well as finding time for the process—all of which can be aided by mathematics coaches. But it stands to reason that coaches can help only to the extent to which they understand the reflective process.

What Reflection Does

Reflection seems uncomplicated, but truly purposeful reflection by teachers on their own actions and their students' responses can be a complex undertaking. According to Stronge (2007), of all the various factors of schooling, teachers have the greatest effect on learning. What they teach, how they teach, and how they interact with students determine students' success or failure in learning. Teachers need to think carefully about all of the elements of a lesson and the results of these elements as evidenced in student engagement, involvement, questioning, and achievement. Coaches can assist teachers in identifying these elements and in identifying, clarifying, and verifying related information or data through the reflection process.

Reflection also helps to solidify training and practice related to skills that teachers want to use in their classrooms. Perfecting new skills requires not only practice but also feedback. And feedback requires reflection to determine whether or what to change in future applications of the new skills. This is another area in which coaches can help. Coaches can be particularly helpful following professional development programs, by assisting teachers both in implementing new strategies introduced in professional development sessions and, later, in reflecting on what happened when they tried the new strategies in their classrooms.

Another aspect of reflection is affirmation. Teachers who are attempting to change—to implement aligned curriculum content, to introduce new strategies into their practice—need reassurance that their efforts are making a difference. Teachers' professional practice and students' achievement often exemplify cause and effect. As teachers work smarter, based on reflections about curriculum and instruction, students learn better and achieve to higher goals. Teachers need to have a strong sense of efficacy. According to Stronge (2007), this sense of efficacy is an important characteristic of effective teachers. Coaches can add to this sense of efficacy and encourage teachers by highlighting evidence of success and acknowledging their work.

Research on Reflection

Research supports mathematics coaches using reflection with teachers. Garmston and Wellman (1999) discuss the effective functioning of groups and note that groups that are too busy to take time to reflect are too busy to improve. It is reasonable to assume that this is true for individuals as well as groups and that educators are no exception. Reflection supports change initiatives through individuals and groups. Reflection also informs practice so that instructional decisions can be made that help students learn. These instructional decisions help to move learning theory into classroom practice (York-Barr, Sommers, Ghere, & Montie, 2001).

Effective teachers have high expectations for students and work to provide students with opportunities to meet them (Stronge, 2007; York-Barr et al., 2001). These high expectations are coupled with a strong sense of teacher efficacy. Teachers who are confident in their abilities to teach are more likely to find that students master required knowledge and skills. Of course, research also suggests that the reverse is true: Low expectations engender poor performance and lack of mastery.

Program implementation with fidelity to a design often aligns with student success (National Research Council [NRC], 2004b). Effective implementation depends on schools supporting such programs. Coaches, teachers, and others who participate in reflection on teaching and learning encourage support for programs that achieve positive results.

Finally, teachers who believe that (1) all students can learn mathematics and (2) they, teachers, are well equipped to teach them will teach successfully—and the students will learn. Reflective practices assist teachers in accepting beliefs such as that mental models and mind-sets can be changed and that differentiated teacher behaviors are required to meet the learning needs of diverse students.

PROCESS FOR ANALYSIS AND REFLECTION

Reflection takes varying amounts of time. Some reflective phases can be stopped and restarted at a later date or time, while other phases cannot. Mathematics coaches and teachers do not have infinite time for lengthy reflective processes but need to set aside sufficient time to achieve a comfortable balance that includes reflection along with collaborative planning, professional conversations, and other activities that promote change and improvement.

Effective analysis and reflection require honesty, which holds true even if teachers are engaged only in self-reflective practice. When other teachers or mathematics coaches are involved, analysis and reflection also require trust.

How lesson outcomes are expressed can be a cue for mathematics coaches to teachers' thinking. If problems with a lesson are persistently attributed to materials, students, schedules, or other things beyond teachers' control, then a first step will be to work on teachers' mind-sets. Dweck (2006) sees many teachers as working from a "fixed" mind-set, one of insecurity. Teachers who feel insecure in their teaching need special care. Until rapport is established, mathematics coaches will not be trusted, and analysis will fall short. Reflection can be a wedge to open the door gradually to honest self-assessment and analysis of lesson outcomes.

Teachers need to understand—and firmly believe—that their actions affect and in many cases determine students' learning. While it may be painful to acknowledge this role when students fail to learn, it is this understanding that builds teachers' sense of efficacy. Efficacy is a characteristic of highly effective teachers. When teachers accept this responsibility for students' learning, they are prepared to be honest with themselves and others, which translates into useful analyses and reflections that lead to improved teaching and learning.

The process of analysis and reflection can best be understood in inter-related phases, often with the next phase building on the previous one. The phases include the following:

1. Analysis of the lesson.

2. Reflection on the lesson.

3. Results of student work.

4. Decisions about intervention.

5. Recording and planning.

This order is useful but not set in stone. In many cases mathematics coaches and teachers will not be able to complete all of the phases in one sitting. Various phases can be emphasized at different sessions or for different lessons.

Another factor that mathematics coaches may want to consider is the planning sequence that we discussed previously: setting the stage, exploration, and summarization. It may be useful to focus analysis and reflection on only one part of this sequence, depending on the lesson, the content, students' reactions, teachers' concerns, or other factors. Following are descriptions of the five phases.

Analysis of the Lesson

Analysis requires a dispassionate look at a lesson, recalling not only what happened but also how what happened related to what was planned.

As much as possible, opinions and emotions should be removed from analysis. The effort should be objective rather than judgmental. Following are some guiding questions that mathematics coaches might pose during this phase:

- What was the lesson goal?
- What were the major lesson segments?
- What did you expect students to do during each segment?
- What did students do during each segment?
- Did the lesson flow as planned?
- Did the lesson require modifications? If so, were the modifications minor, moderate, or major?
- What were the changes by segment?

Linking teachers' actions to students' learning will occur during reflection. Thus, an accurate picture of the lesson is essential groundwork. However, reflection can be delayed if it seems appropriate, for example, to consider the results of students' work or other matters beforehand. Mathematics coaches and teachers also may choose to focus on only one part of the lesson, such as exploration. Building the analysis and reflection process should match the needs of the teachers and students.

An accurate description of a classroom and the events that occurred during a lesson means that teachers are less able to gloss over parts of the lesson that did not go well and will help teachers become more aware of what students were actually doing, or not doing, during the lesson. For example, if teachers continually recall that students were "listening," "being quiet," "sitting," "watching," or were in other ways disengaged, then they will come to realize a need to try strategies that increase students' active involvement.

As teachers engage in analysis over time, they will enhance their ability to recall classroom events and to recognize coherence and discord when examining whether the planned lesson was the taught lesson. This enhanced capacity for analysis is a positive step in the improvement of teaching and learning.

Reflection on the Lesson

This phase of the process often is the one that mathematics coaches and teachers want to "hurry up and get to," because it focuses on the results of a lesson. It answers the questions What did students do in response to what I (the teacher) did? Did the lesson work?

This is a form of action research, whether teachers think of it that way or not. Teachers inquire into lesson design, lesson delivery, and student learning. In planning the lesson, teachers selected specific content for students to learn and instructional strategies that they believed would convey that content. They also chose assessments that would confirm whether students understood the content and could apply the necessary skills or procedures to a related task or set of tasks. Reflection considers all of these lesson components and helps teachers deliberate about ways to refine their lessons.

Following are some questions that mathematics coaches may use to encourage reflection:

- Did students appear to have misconceptions about any particular part of the lesson?
- What actions did you take? Why did you select these actions?
- How were students participating during the various lesson segments?
- Did the lesson achieve the desired learning objective?
- What evidence do you have that the lesson objective was achieved?

During a lesson, teachers sometimes see a need to modify the lesson plan. If this has occurred, the coach may want to ask these questions:

- What were your cues that the lesson needed changing?
- What were the results of these changes?

Mathematics coaches should remember that teachers may feel vulnerable during the reflective phase. They care about their students, and they realize the importance of the instructional strategies they select. If the lesson does not go as planned or if students fail to learn, then teachers may blame themselves for not better preparing for, anticipating, or reacting to the learning challenges. Effective teachers tend to be self-critical. This self-criticism comes from a true desire to improve, a deep concern for students, and a belief in efficacy. For effective teachers this translates into recognizing that if the students did not learn, then the teachers must not have taken appropriate action. This characteristic often becomes apparent during the reflective process and needs to be carefully handled by mathematics coaches, so that self-criticism becomes a positive trait rather than a detriment to improvement.

A different problem arises when teachers are insufficiently self-aware or self-critical. Rather than look to the analysis for guidance in reflection, they may judge a lesson's success or failure solely on how well students behaved. Obviously, this is a generalization and should to be taken as such. But mathematics coaches must be alert to how teachers view the lesson and their role in it. Coaches cannot assume that effective teachers do not need assistance and support for reflective practice. Nor can coaches simply give general directions to less effective teachers and assume that they will discover much of value as they think about a lesson.

Results of Student Work

Studying student work can bolster the analysis phase or the reflection phase. It also can be used as a launch for either of these phases. When they examine student work, mathematics coaches assist teachers by reinforcing the value of analyzing lesson delivery and reflecting on the results of a lesson. Was reverse planning used? Did the assessment chosen prior to teaching the lesson reveal strengths and weakness in instruction? What were students able to do successfully? What proved challenging? What were students unable to do?

Studying the results of student work should lead teachers to answer two questions:

- What alternative instructional strategies might have increased students' learning during the lesson?
- What strategies might be used in future to help students learn content or skills that they did not master in the lesson as taught?

Mathematics coaches may find some of the following questions useful to assist teachers in thinking about the tasks they posed in the lesson:

- What did you expect students to say, write, or do?
- Which paper is an example of an average understanding of the lesson? What did the student do on the paper that indicates understanding?
- Which paper is an example of exceptional understanding? What did the student do that makes the work exceptional?
- Which paper is an example that looks like the student did not understand the lesson? What did the student fail to do or understand?

Decisions About Intervention

These questions can help provide additional clarity about the effectiveness of the lesson and possible next steps to be taken:

- What is the range of understanding demonstrated by student work?
- What would an unsuccessful student need to do to become an average student?

- What could an average student do to become exceptional?
- What knowledge or skills were taught in the lesson? What were pre-requisite knowledge and skills?
- What might have been done during the lesson to help students be more successful? What will help students who did not understand this lesson to learn the content and skills in the future?
- Might intervention in future lessons use content and skills reviews or scaffolding?
- Should such intervention be integrated into future lessons, or should intervention be conducted outside of the classroom?
- How do you intend to provide this feedback to the students?

The last question gets at a particularly important aspect of studying student work—namely, giving feedback to students about their performance. According to Marzano (2003), "In fact, a review of almost 8,000 studies led John Hattie (1992) to comment, 'The most powerful single modification that enhances achievement is feedback'" (p. 37). He further found that feedback, to be effective, must be timely and specific to the content being taught and learned. Mathematics coaches need to help teachers realize that changes in instructional strategies and expectations must involve students. If students understand what is expected of them, then they are more likely to perform well. This directly relates to the reverse planning process in which, for instance, students review the unit test and preview content prior to the start of a new unit or lesson.

Recording and Planning

With multiple teaching assignments, memory alone is not sufficient. Creating a record of analysis and reflection will help ensure that ideas are not lost and can be incorporated into future lesson planning. Mathematics coaches should encourage teachers to respond to the following question: When you next teach this lesson, what do you want to remember to do differently?

The recorded answer should be stated so that it will be understood as readily a year later as a week later. Of course, what teachers learn during analysis and reflection will be used more than once a year. A clear record also forms a catalog of ideas for improving similar lessons or lessons that use related skills or deal with related content. As teachers refine their strategies, such records become living documents, chronicling teachers' changes in content understandings and their growing repertoire of instructional strategies.

STRUCTURES FOR REFLECTION

Teachers and mathematics coaches need multiple ways to structure reflection. A school that has professional learning communities as part of its collaborative structure is in an excellent position to encourage reflective practice. But regardless of the organization of a school or the types of collaboration that exist, coaches will need to engage teachers in one-on-one professional conversations. Mathematics coaches can be instrumental in helping teachers, principals, and others understand and use the following ways to structure reflection.

Individual Reflection

Teachers need to practice self-reflection as part of ongoing, individual, professional improvement. While individual reflection may seem to be the easiest and least complicated starting point for reflective practice, teachers will need assistance to learn how to use effective reflection. A day of inservice training or a list of questions is insufficient. Mathematics coaches must be mindful that individual teachers will differ in their capacity for self-reflection. Some will need more guidance than others to use the five phases described in this chapter.

Coach–Teacher Reflection

For many teachers a successful starting point is to engage in reflection with a mathematics coach. Reflection can be woven into other collaborative work, such as coplanning. Including some form of reflection on a previous lesson when planning a future lesson is logical.

Peer–Peer Reflection

When teachers are comfortable with reflection and peer collaboration, they may be encouraged to reflect on lessons with a colleague. This may involve the teachers co-reflecting on a common lesson, or one teacher may serve as a reflective guide for the other. Either approach can work, but if one teacher is acting as the coach, then typical coaching techniques should be used, such as active listening and asking reflective questions.

Group Reflection

If several teachers teach a common lesson, then group reflection is an option. Professional learning communities can use this reflective practice, but this is not the same as lesson study. Group reflection does not continue to use and perfect the same lesson, which is done in lesson study.

Group reflection is intended to improve teaching and learning by providing coherence to lesson design and delivery. It also involves peer pressure, shared experience, and shared learning. Teachers work together to identify, design, and deliver effective lessons that reach a learning objective for the greatest number of students.

According to Youngs and King (2002), learning communities have several characteristics that relate to group reflection:

> A strong schoolwide professional community is characterized by (a) shared goals for student learning; (b) meaningful collaboration among faculty members; (c) in-depth inquiry into assumptions, evidence, and alternative solutions to problems; and (d) opportunities for teachers to exert influence over their work. (p. 646)

Mathematics coaches can use this list to guide group reflection.

Department Reflection

This type of reflection can help teachers remember that they are part of a professional team. Department reflections take samples of student work (unacceptable, acceptable, and exemplary), remove students' names, and review work across subjects and courses. Department members look for patterns among students' misconceptions with the goal of determining (1) how the misconceptions might have developed and (2) how they can be corrected. Mathematics coaches can assist by helping teachers study curriculum and strategies so that misconceptions can be avoided in the future.

Department reflection is an excellent way to view progress over time and to view the coherence of various courses. Misconceptions may arise from curriculum alignment problems. Through department reflection, teachers may discover, for example, that there is a gap in state content standards or in instructional materials. Or teachers may decide that they need to embed more opportunities for students to apply concepts or to reinforce them through scaffolding.

All of these reflection structures can be useful, and mathematics coaches can ensure that they are conducted successfully.

CRITICAL POINTS

Reflection involves the following five phases:

Analysis: What took place during the lesson? What did the teacher do? What did students do?

Reflection: What were the outcomes of the lesson? What teacher actions influenced student actions?

Student Work: What were students able to do successfully? What were they challenged by or unable to do?

Intervention: What does the teacher plan to do to correct students' misunderstandings?

Recording: What does the teacher need to remember to improve the lesson in the future?

9 Charting Long-Term Progress

The information in this book is designed to assist mathematics coaches in developing short- and long-term improvement plans. Coaches work with teachers and school leaders to determine the type of mathematics program desired. A high-quality mathematics program will be based on National Council of Teachers of Mathematics (NCTM) principles of equity, curriculum, teaching, learning, assessment, and technology. Short-term goals usually aim to increase learning by current students, helping them succeed in their current classes and setting a foundation so that they can continue into advanced mathematics.

Mathematics improvement goes beyond the current students. It is also a long-term goal, with the idea that fundamental improvement accomplished incrementally will change mathematics teaching and learning for the better in the future. In this chapter we take up the question of how mathematics coaches, teachers, and others ascertain that long-term improvement is being accomplished. Charting progress over the long term requires data. Some groundwork for this chapter was laid in Chapter 5. Much of the data collected to assess progress over the short term also will be valuable to maintain over the long term.

TREND DATA

Using data effectively is a characteristic of effective schools (Reeves, 2006). Data acquired with consistency over time is called trend data. Trend data works to transform, not merely inform, instruction. Much of the data collection previously discussed was concerned with helping teachers make informed decisions based on performance by students in their classes. These data help teachers decide what to do in response to what students have or have not learned. Such data are immediately useful in planning. This use of data is an additive approach, meaning that new content and skills are incorporated into already established routines, actions, and beliefs.

By contrast, trend data are used to support transformative learning, in which deeply held beliefs are changed (Kaser, Mundry, Stiles, & Loucks-Horsley, 2002). Trend data provide evidence that positive changes are being made over time. Teachers may feel pressure to use a new curriculum, unfamiliar strategies, or newly adopted textbooks; but changes in what and how they teach will not become routine until they believe in them. Data that clearly demonstrate the effectiveness of new approaches bolster teachers' efforts to change.

Mathematics coaches are not solely responsible for trend data. School principals and curriculum coordinators often collect and analyze data. Effective principals and curriculum leaders use trend data to support teachers and indicate progress on school- or district-level reform (Spillane et al., 2002). However, mathematics coaches will need to work closely with teachers, explaining data and helping teachers understand how best to use this information to shape lesson planning and instruction.

WHY EMPHASIZE TREND DATA?

Coaching is a complex endeavor, and mathematics coaches may struggle with the idea of trend data as opposed to concentrating on immediate-feedback data used to inform instruction. In reality both data sets inform instruction. Coaches may be coordinating mathematics teachers' efforts in analyzing common assessments (benchmarks) and reviewing year-end data generated from state assessments. But while these are vital activities for developing a high-quality mathematics program, they are not sufficient for plotting a course for long-term improvement. For this overarching purpose, coaches need to collect and examine data that indicate whether

- students are reaching increasingly higher levels of mathematics achievement,
- teachers are obtaining a sense of efficacy, and
- progress is being made toward a consistently high-quality mathematics program.

These goals can be assessed only by using trend data, and each of these goals merits further discussion.

Students Reaching Higher Levels of Achievement

As mentioned previously, many schools have long operated from a belief that mathematics ability is a gift from birth. Mathematical ability is either in the genes or it is not (Dweck, 2006). If not, there are ample opportunities and careers available that do not require mastery of mathematics beyond basic computation. Based on this belief, the curriculum has allowed students who do not do well in mathematics to avoid the subject in large part beyond the eighth grade.

This approach is no longer viable. Education leaders across the board now recognize that mastery of challenging content and skills must be the floor rather than the ceiling when it comes to mathematics learning. Many states have revised graduation requirements accordingly to include more mathematics. At the same time, many districts, individual schools, and mathematics teachers have maintained old beliefs and resisted efforts to increase mathematics achievement for all students.

Support for more mathematics and higher levels of conceptual understanding has a basis in research (Achieve, 2006). Today high school diplomas are not the end of educational achievement but the beginning for increasingly larger numbers of students. Most new jobs require further education, and the extent of required education is only likely to increase (Achieve, 2006). Mathematics is a key to successful postsecondary education and provides learners with flexibility in choosing future careers.

Routine assessments and even state-level assessments do not indicate whether more students are enrolling in higher-level mathematics courses or if they are being successful in these courses. To answer these questions, trend data are necessary.

Teachers Obtaining a Sense of Efficacy

Beliefs that only some students could learn mathematics well and that mathematics, while important for some, was not essential for all students have worked to form current instructional practices in many mathematics classrooms (National Research Council [NRC], 2002). By adopting these beliefs, mathematics teachers greatly diminished their sense of professional efficacy. Teachers need support from mathematics coaches to change their instructional methods. They need to understand that what they do indeed matters when it comes to students' learning. By regaining a sense of efficacy, teachers can adopt the belief that all students can learn mathematics (Stronge, 2007). Conzemius and O'Neill (2001) state it this way:

Education is not just about methods and textbooks; it's about being able to demonstrate through student performance that the instruction provided has resulted in learning. . . . Teachers' sense of efficacy is tightly linked with a high degree of professional engagement. Tschannen-Moran and colleagues (1998) note, "The perception that a performance has been successful affects the effort [teachers] put into teaching, the goals they set, and their level of aspiration. . . ." Teachers feel a profound sense of accomplishment when they know their instructional efforts have translated into learning. . . . They know that what they are doing is making a difference. Without the feedback data provide, teachers can only guess (and hope) that their students have achieved the desired outcomes. (p. 47)

While classroom data are important to a sense of efficacy, trend data support a collaborative belief critical to substantive, schoolwide change. It is not just "me and my students" but everyone and all students. This sense of efficacy is derived from evidence of steady progress. A sense of accomplishment does not have to come from dramatic results; evidence that the school is moving forward is sufficient (Schmoker, 1999). The idea of accomplished performance increases self-esteem and provides the confidence to work harder to achieve even greater goals (Fullan, 1993).

Progress Toward a High-Quality Program

Trend data help teachers and mathematics coaches step back from intense daily work to observe progress over time. Mathematics coaches must form a clear picture of a high-quality mathematics program with factors about progress that they can discuss with teachers. While it is certainly desirable to have more students pass state assessments each year, data sets from these sources are too narrow for determining whether a mathematics program is improving. Each NCTM principle needs to be addressed when charting progress:

Equity: Mathematics coaches want to know that all students are provided access to high-quality mathematics programs. No barriers prevent students from participating in deeper, richer mathematics. An example of a barrier to equity is ability tracking that preselects in elementary school the students who will be successful in high school.

Curriculum: Mathematics coaches ensure that every mathematics class has well-defined mathematics content that is not limited to basic computation. Mathematics knowledge, skills, and concepts are presented developmentally and are challenging. The curriculum provides teachers with sufficient information, defining the scope and sequence of mathematics content and appropriate strategies.

Teaching: Mathematics coaches ensure that every student has access to inclusive instructional strategies that encourage and promote student participation. Regardless of their assigned teachers, students are given opportunities to learn appropriate content. Teachers understand the degree of influence they exert on students and the effect they have on learning.

Learning: Mathematics coaches ensure that students are given opportunities to explore, think, reason, and solve challenging problems that show mathematics to be reasonable and applicable. Students know what mathematics they are expected to learn and are provided data to support their progress in learning it. Students are given multiple ways and opportunities to learn recommended content by working independently, with partners, in small groups, and in whole-group settings.

Assessment: Mathematics coaches ensure that students have opportunities to justify and strengthen their own understanding of mathematical concepts. Students see the developmental nature of mathematics, understand the organizational methods used for introducing concepts, and know their progress in learning required concepts. Assessments are more than just a grade to be recorded. Assessments assist students in reflecting on their learning and in self-correcting misconceptions.

Technology: Mathematics coaches ensure equal access to mathematical tools, such as calculators, computers, and data-collecting and processing devices. Technology is not used merely to perform calculations but as a vital tool to explore complex mathematical situations.

Mathematics classrooms must be (or become) places where teacher practices "focus on sense-making, self-assessment, and reflection on what worked and what needs improving" (NRC, 2000, p. 12). Teachers need to recognize and comprehend students' preexisting understandings before they can push students into new areas of mathematics (Cushman, 2003; NRC, 2000). Trend data can be used to point the way toward progress in all of these areas.

INDICATORS OF SUCCESS

Most trend data are not different from data already being collected. But trend data are charted differently. Mathematics coaches should not collect data from teachers for trends if such data are already being collected in some other way.

Many indicators can signal positive trends, among them are

- Student achievement is increasing on state assessments.
- Higher percentages of students are obtaining higher scores on benchmarks.
- Performance gaps among subgroups are decreasing.
- Students' thinking is more visible on open-response items.
- More students are in the "exemplary" and "acceptable" performance categories.
- More students are taking more mathematics courses.
- More students are enrolling in higher-level mathematics courses.
- Students are receiving higher grades in mathematics courses and there are fewer failing students.
- Greater consistency and coherence are observed in instructional practices.
- Professional meetings with mathematics coaches and among teachers are efficient, effective, and focused on improvement.
- Ethnic diversity is apparent in mathematics classes.

These indicators require data from assessments, classroom observations, class schedules, and other sources.

USING TREND DATA TO INFORM TEACHING

Teachers and mathematics coaches use assessment data to inform instruction for prompt changes in strategies that are designed to improve students' learning. There may be a number of reasons why students have difficulty with particular lessons. Fine-tuning a lesson and preparing for interventions are important tasks for teachers throughout the school year. But there also is a larger picture. If students repeatedly demonstrate weakness in certain units or lessons, then broader adjustments should be made. Such major changes should be supported by trend data.

Mathematics coaches use cross-referenced data to help identify problem areas in the mathematics curriculum. Perhaps a larger than usual number of students is receiving lower grades for a particular unit, or a state assessment shows that many students are struggling with certain concepts. These are reasons to investigate what is happening.

When investigating why students are not performing up to expectations, a primary question is whether the skills or content actually are included in the state standards. For example, the content in question might be a leftover from an earlier curriculum that teachers have been reluctant to give up. This is an alignment issue. Is the content being taught the content that is intended to be taught?

Learning materials may be another issue. Are they misaligned with the content intended to be taught? For example, students may not be performing well on measurement. On investigation the mathematic coach discovers that the textbook emphasizes linear measurement, whereas the curriculum emphasizes liquid measurement. Teachers will need supplementary materials to teach the intended content.

Pacing and sequence are other potential problem areas. Does the content flow logically? Are appropriate prerequisites taught prior to introducing new content and skills? Coaches may need to investigate what is taught in earlier grades to answer questions about prerequisite skills. Is more instructional time needed for students to master certain concepts or skills? Perhaps teachers need to provide more opportunities for practice.

Coaches and teachers know that misconceptions interfere with learning. If some skills are counterintuitive to students' reasoning, then it will take greater effort for teachers to correct misconceptions. For example, second- and third-grade students learn that multiplication of whole numbers is the same as repeated addition. In all cases except those with 0 and 1 as factors, a product is greater than the factors. When multiplication of fractions is introduced in later grades, many students reason that the product of two fractions must always be greater than either of the factors:

$$3 \times 4 = 12 \text{ so } 12 > 3 \text{ and } 12 > 4;$$

$$1/2 \times 1/3 = 1/6 \text{ but } 1/6 < 1/2 \text{ and } 1/6 < 1/3.$$

Additional effort may be required for teachers to explain these conflicting ideas so that students fully understand the concepts. Coaches and teachers may need to create their own teaching notes to ensure effectiveness. Effective materials do exist, but as the National Research Council (2002) points out, "Instructional materials need to have teacher notes that support teachers' understandings of mathematical concepts, student thinking and student errors, and effective pedagogical supports and techniques" (p. 28). Supplying teachers with additional reminders about teaching a particular concept or skill might be necessary.

Some problems confirmed in trend data may be obvious and easy to fix. Others may be complex and difficult, if not impossible, to solve. For example, there may be a subtle bias in a lesson or in materials that interferes with understanding. This bias may not be readily apparent to coaches or teachers. Mathematics coaches may need to talk with some of the students who missed certain problems and ask them to explain their thinking. Then coaches may need to talk with some students who correctly solved the problems and ask them to explain their thinking. This is labor intensive but may lead to a solution, or coaches may need to devise several instructional approaches and ask teachers to experiment to determine which approach works best.

DATA SOURCES AND DISPLAYS

Numerous data sources can be investigated to observe trends. How data are displayed and the degree of refinement of the data will directly reflect the size of a school or department. Coaches need trend data to be refined enough to be meaningful but not individualized. Building rapport and maintaining confidentiality argue against greater specificity, especially in the case of small or specialized classes. For example, if there is only one calculus teacher with one class of 15 students, then posting failure rates and progress would be intrusive and inappropriate.

An initial data source that coaches will find useful is benchmark assessments. Coaches can select an appropriate measure to display on a chart. The data may be average grade or percent passing for a course. Mathematics coaches also may elect to display examples of both acceptable and unacceptable student work (without students' or teachers' names). Doing so will be similar to creating a portfolio to show how students refine their understanding during a course.

In some cases mathematics coaches should meet with all of the teachers of a particular grade or course, or the entire mathematics department, and gather work samples from common assessments that can be displayed and discussed. Discussing students' papers or tests is a valuable exercise for coaches and teachers.

Mathematics coaches also may want to display passing rates for classes for each grading period. The purpose is to observe whether the passing rate increases. Results might be recorded as follows:

Algebra I

First grading period: 77% passing

Second grading period: 79% passing

Third grading period: 82% passing

Fourth grading period: 83% passing

Another data set might be the number of students enrolled by course.

Mathematics coaches also could chart students' progress on state assessments. Depending on how data are organized, coaches may be able to develop a comparison chart over time. Here is an example:

Percentage of Fifth-Grade Students Passing the State Mathematics Assessment

Year	Concepts	Geometry	Measurement	Problem Solving
2005	56	73	82	64
2006	61	75	82	68
2007	65	78	85	74

Coaches should remember that data are to be used to encourage and support staff in their efforts to improve; data should be carrots, not sticks. With this encouragement and support in mind, mathematics coaches may choose to keep data refinement to a minimum.

Baseline data allow coaches to meet with teachers to set challenging but realistic goals for student success. Coaches must take the leadership role, understanding that it is unrealistic for teachers to move students from 10% passing the state assessment to 90% passing in one year. But it is equally unrealistic to set a goal of moving students from 10% passing to 11% passing. Mathematics coaches work with teachers to select reasonable goals and identify corresponding benchmarks along the way.

USING TREND DATA FOR PROFESSIONAL DEVELOPMENT

Trend data also can assist mathematics coaches and teachers in recognizing specific professional development needs, which may focus on particular units, materials, content, or strategies.

Effective professional development, like classroom instruction, depends on transferring knowledge into practice. Teachers must take skills and knowledge obtained through professional learning back to the classroom. For example, if the goal is to increase students' passing rates on state assessments, then professional development must be based on trend data that identify problem areas and must teach research-based strategies aligned to the content in question.

Trend data help mathematics coaches and teachers understand a bigger picture of change and create a vision of manageable improvement. Change can be overwhelming and frustrating. This is particularly true if it appears not to have a clear purpose or a way to measure success. The bottom line is that mathematics coaches are in a position to step back from the day-to-day routines of teaching and focus on data. What the facts say provides impetus for mathematics coaches to act as leaders while teachers work to improve teaching and learning.

CRITICAL POINTS

In moving classroom instruction from "what is" to "what needs to be," mathematics coaches must identify observable guideposts and monitor progress. Trend data are essential for these purposes when it comes to long-term improvement and change that takes time.

Part III

Continuing
the Work

10 Working Within the Education System

Mathematics coaches are ready to step back and view the big picture—the system in which coaches and teachers operate. Coaches are obligated to work effectively within the entire system, not just within specific schools or with certain teachers. But that obligation may be implicit and imprecise, depending on the coaches' job description.

Sustainable change must in some ways be systemic, which means that on some level mathematics coaches must gain cooperation from everyone in the education system who is involved in working with students. Cooperation and collaboration help to focus on changes that improve teaching and learning, and cooperation begins with communication. In effective organizations people are able to communicate with one another when necessary, without adhering to traditional vertical or horizontal patterns (Short & Greer, 2002).

But just as a lack of job clarity and failure to build professional rapport with teachers can undermine coaches' efforts to improve teaching and learning, so can misunderstandings or erroneous expectations about the school system and how it operates. In many cases such misunderstandings arise from inadequate or unrealistic ideas about power—the coaches' power to effect change and the power of others to support or undermine that change. Individuals who feel they do not possess the power to make a difference will not supply the energy needed to make and sustain change.

Our purpose in this chapter is to explore the idea that power in an education system equates to influence. Communication networks are spheres of influence. Within a school system, there are layers of formal and informal communication—networks with all degrees and types of influence shared among and between school personnel. Successful mathematics coaches recognize, identify, and locate these networks and use them to facilitate professional conversations and maintain coherence in the change effort.

Influence is not the only dynamic that affects change initiatives. Teachers' jobs are stressful and demanding. Merely to maintain what they have takes all their energy. Additional energy to change a system is not going to come from teachers working in relative isolation from one another. This is why coaching and teaming are important. Coaches add energy to the change formula. Synergy from learning communities also can add energy. These combined forces can transform classrooms. But lack of trust can just as easily undermine and drain energy.

Collaborative planning and coteaching are methods for building trust with classroom teachers. Trust does not end there, however. When mathematics coaches are trusted and building principals are not, change will be difficult to sustain. Mathematics coaches cannot work in isolation any more than teachers can. The role of mathematics coaches places them in positions to work in collegial relationships with principals and central office staff as well as with teachers. Sustainable change will require attention to working effectively at multiple levels of the education system.

THE GREAT DIVIDE

Educators who have spent time as classroom teachers recognize that a chasm often exists between schools and the central office—"the great divide." A sense of "us versus them" may be pervasive, in spite of communication efforts by central office staff to convey the message that they are there to help and provide support.

Principals normally cross this divide on a regular basis, often through weekly meetings and planning sessions at the central office. As a result they sometimes are in a precarious situation. Effective principals buffer teachers from unnecessary intrusions that disrupt or take time away from teaching and learning or drain teachers' energies. Principals often see a need—or are asked by teachers—to protect the school from central office mandates that teachers view as unnecessary or intrusive.

The view from the central office is quite different. Central office staff sometimes see principals as obstacles to school improvement initiatives.

These district-level administrators may see their jobs as complicated and frustrated by principals' lack of action. Principals sometimes are told that they are to be instructional leaders in their schools, but the central office often dominates that role. Conflicts arise, and those on both sides of the great divide are partly right and partly wrong most of the time.

Short and Greer (2002) comment that "in the eyes of central office officials who are in charge of selecting principals, 'good' principals can be trusted to carry out the central office directions, explain and sell the central office point of view, and always ask for directions from their supervisors when facing a new situation" (p. 67). But many district-level administrators have not worked as principals and do not grasp the complexity of the principalship.

Mathematics coaches need to understand two important things. First, in terms of supervisory power, few central office administrators have authority over principals. Usually only the superintendent and an assistant superintendent function as line supervisors of the principals in a school district. Second, principals' workdays are hectic and demanding. Short and Greer (2002) note that "According to the school effectiveness literature, 80% of the typical principals' day consists of conversations of 2 minutes or less" (p. 66).

Why is this information important to mathematics coaches? Following are some points to consider:

- Mathematics coaches are not classroom teachers. Which side of the great divide are coaches on?
- Mathematics coaches work in schools with teachers, but who are their supervisors? Building principals? Mathematics coordinators or curriculum directors? Both? Others? Must coaches follow principals' directives?
- Who ultimately is responsible for student performance? If coaches identify content or strategies as okay and principals view them as not okay, to whom should teachers listen?
- How do mathematics coaches fit into the 20% of principals' days that are not just two-minute conversations? Or can they?

Exact answers may be impossible and certainly will not be universal. It will be up to mathematics coaches to attempt to answer these questions if they hope to do their jobs well.

MANAGEMENT VERSUS LEADERSHIP

People who feel powerless do not change their habits nor do they change the habits of others. Educators feel powerless when they believe their actions have no effect. Thus, a key role for mathematics coaches will be to ensure that teachers and others with whom they work, including administrators, feel empowered.

Power can be and often is misunderstood in relation to management and leadership. Management and leadership skills are both needed for an effective education system. But management tasks often seem to be easier to understand and perform, and so they tend to be the default approach. Managers often operate from an authoritative, top-down perspective, using negative power—"my way or the highway." Performance, whether what teachers do or what students learn, is rated by a checklist rather than by hard-to-quantify results, and compliance with rules is considered the critical factor. However, educators cannot "manage" their way into effective schools. Regulation seldom leads to innovation or positive change.

Leadership does produce positive results, but it is more complicated than management. Leaders must master not only a full range of content and skills but also the nuances of power and the influences that affect leadership initiatives but may lie beyond leaders' ability to control. The true power of a leader is influence, and the degree of influence leaders hold and can exercise is based on trust.

Mathematics coaches are instructional leaders, though they may assume, incorrectly, that power is structured to match the established hierarchy of the education system—and their positions have none. However, leadership influence equates to real power when it comes to performing the job they were hired to do—namely, to improve teaching and learning.

Leadership Styles

Leadership takes many forms. There are formal and informal leaders by designation, by default, and by force of personality and trust. Leaders operate using one or more styles, often choosing among styles to achieve desired outcomes.

A great deal of literature on leadership styles exists. We have chosen to draw on two resources: the work of Goleman in 2002 from the Institute for Management Excellence (2008) and the work of Lewin in 1939 from *Changing Minds* (2008). Mathematics coaches may wish to pursue this topic in more depth. A list of the six leadership styles developed by Goleman can be found in Resource D. The list provides examples of clarifying statements as well as the relationships to power domains.

In an attempt to uncomplicate a complicated issue, we will take up only the three leadership styles identified by Lewin as autocratic, democratic, and laissez-faire.

Autocratic leaders simply make decisions. They do not bother to ask for, nor do they take, input. These leaders do not consult with interested or affected parties. Autocratic leadership, according to Lewin, causes the greatest discontent.

Autocratic leaders can be transparent, meaning that their messages are readily understood. Mathematics coaches probably will not be able to change this type of leader. At best they can work with these leaders' clarity. When autocratic leaders are unclear, problems are compounded by uncertainty when attempting to interpret what such leaders require. Under autocratic leadership, only a few lines of communication are needed to disseminate the leader's messages. The formal lines run one way, from leaders down the chain. In this case mathematics coaches can work to strengthen informal lines of communication, determine the tolerance level of leaders toward having communication networks, and serve as partners for teachers otherwise operating in isolation.

Democratic leaders employ a participatory style of leadership. People likely to be affected are involved in making decisions even though these leaders may make the final decisions. Most democratic leaders attempt to reach consensus. As a result this leadership style tends to be preferred and appreciated by those involved with such leaders.

Mathematics coaches are well positioned to be part of a team when working with democratic leaders. They can provide team members with needed information and serve as resources in other ways. While democratic leadership is a preferred style, poor or erroneous decisions still can be made. Thus, mathematics coaches can play a role in ensuring the use of correct information and accurate interpretation and implementation of it, such as using sound data to guide instructional decisions. Communication networks—formal and informal—tend to thrive under democratic leaders. An important activity for mathematics coaches under this leadership style is ensuring that everyone is hooked into at least one network.

Laissez-faire leaders attempt to minimize their involvement in making decisions. In general those who are involved with this type of leader make their own decisions. A benefit of this style may be that mathematics coaches have opportunities to work with small groups of teachers and feel truly empowered along with those in the groups. Group members gather data, analyze problems, offer solutions, and decide courses of action. In many cases one responsibility of mathematics coaches will be making sure that group decisions are transparent to such leaders.

Laissez-faire leaders may have numerous formal and informal networks in operation, but the leaders may not be part of some of the networks. Coaches need to work with formal networks to locate people actually making decisions and to determine what decisions are being made. They also must work to bring these decision-makers' laissez-faire leaders into the decision-making process.

Other styles of leadership are discussed in the education literature, but these three styles broadly encompass the various other styles. Whatever the leadership style, mathematics coaches must work to form strong working relationships with leaders and to understand the positions of teachers.

INFLUENCE AS POWER

One of the positive steps that mathematics coaches can take is to help teachers understand their power as a factor of the influence they exert over what and how they teach and, in consequence, what and how well students learn.

For example, teachers are able to manage their classrooms with management power as well as to provide leadership influence. Coaches need to realize that they themselves have the same power and more, because they have more contacts with more people at various levels of the education system. Coaches also have power through their influence on teachers in terms of content alignment and the introduction of highly effective instructional strategies.

Power sometimes conveys negative connotations. These arise from misuses of power or influence. The "power" to influence constructive change is positive.

Domains of Power

A way for instructional leaders to think about power is through established "domains of power." Messages transmitted through verbal and nonverbal communications also involve the power bases of the communicators. There are many domains, or forms, of power, some inherent to various official positions, others arising from the characteristics of the leader. These domains can be summarized as shown in Figure 10.1.

Careful analysis of the power domains in Figure 10.1 reveals only one traditional understanding of power—the power of position. All of the other powers devolve to individuals through influence. For example, consider the power to reward or punish. This power appears to be fairly straightforward. Teachers, students, and people in general may be controlled by the power of others either to reward or to punish them for certain actions. Those with such power range from supervisors to court judges. But unless the rewards or punishments are valued, either desired or feared, people may not change what they do, whether that means working harder or obeying the speed limit.

Covey (1991) posits a different idea of power when he states, "Power is the capacity to act, the strength and courage to accomplish something. It

---

Figure 10.1 Domains of Power

Position

This is the power that comes with your job title. This power is awarded to you by the district in the form of policy. It is the chain of command. It is also the legitimate right of the leader, usually by virtue of the position that the leader holds, to prescribe or control behavior.

Knowledge/Expertise

This is the power you possess as information, ability, special knowledge or expertise, or talent. The information may be gained through access or your background experience.

Character

This is your integrity status as perceived by the staff, the degree of trust.

Reward/Recognition or Punishment

This is the power you have as part of your position to make decisions and reward individuals or groups for their effort.

Coercion

This is the power of fear, threat, intimidation, or the control over punishment.

Persuasion

This is the ability to be charismatic or convincing.

Peers

This is the power of groups. It is the need for individuals to belong and socially fit in.

SOURCE: *Ten Types of Power,* n.d.; Short & Greer, 2002, pp. 61–62.

is the vital energy to make choices and decisions" (p. 23). Are influence and energy the same in this case?

Even dictionary definitions of *power* are vague, most blending the ideas of power and influence. Indeed, *influence* often is used as a descriptor of *power,* as in "possession of control, authority, or influence over others." But influence is more about trust and integrity. To have influence, leaders' opinions must be respected and valued. For mathematics coaches, this argues for spending time building rapport through collaborative, collegial activities. Then coaches can persuade teachers to act in certain ways, such as implementing new instructional strategies, because it is the right thing to do, not because it is mandated.

Building Trust

How do mathematics coaches become trustworthy? What are observable actions of a trustworthy person? Short and Greer (2002) state,

> Trust building is a slow process that requires disclosure, authenticity of work and action, follow-through in meeting each other's needs, respect for diversity, enabling teachers to take action in a risk-taking environment without fear of reprisal, and basic ethical actions that demonstrate a concern for the well-being of others. (p. 159)

Teachers form trust at varying rates. When a few teachers accept mathematics coaches as trustworthy and begin to act accordingly, others tend join in until trust fully flourishes (Short & Greer, 2002).

Leadership traits and behaviors that build trust include sending clear, consistent messages with easily understood expectations and goals. Effective organizations are noteworthy for having processes for "communication, goal setting, decision making, conflict management, and problem solving" (Short & Greer, 2002, p. 72). Mathematics coaches who wish to be effective not only will fit into existing formal and informal networks but also will create networks. As they work with teachers, principals, and others, most coaches discover that they are, in fact, altering formal and informal communication networks. Such restructuring should not to be taken lightly. Communicating about communicating is important so that everyone has similar expectations about sending, receiving, and interpreting messages.

Communication, whether by voice, written word, or in person, is always nuanced. Consider face-to-face communication and the effects of body language and other nonverbal communication. According to Garmston and Wellman (1999), "Since the greatest part of communication occurs nonverbally, group members need consciousness about their total communication package. This includes posture, proximity, muscle tension, facial expression, and the pitch, pace, volume, and inflection in their voices" (p. 45).

Finally, there are all the previous encounters between individuals and personal working relationships that have been developed. This is why, on some mornings, a simple "good morning" can be translated in so many ways. Is the person saying "good morning" preoccupied, angry, upset, cheerful, or happy? Is it an announcement about something good that occurred or a wish that something good would occur? Sound ridiculous? Perhaps, but it is true nonetheless.

Transparency

Classroom life is hectic enough for teachers. They do not need to be bombarded with vague, inconsistent messages about expectations, behaviors, and actions. Mathematics coaches need to work with principals and other administrators responsible for content to ensure that communication is as clear and consistent as possible. One of the ways to ensure effective communication is by being "transparent"—that is, working to bring all actions to the forefront, to make them overt. Teachers should not have to guess at what principals or coaches expect them to be doing. Teachers also cannot constantly be forced to guess whether the same expectations are held by mathematics coaches, principals, and central office administrators. Just as curriculum must align, so must expectations. Transparency helps to reduce communication breakdowns by leaving less room for rumor, speculation, and misinterpretation.

Instructional leaders, such as coaches, supervisors, coordinators, and lead teachers, are challenged to move from management—for example, as "documenter" of compliance—to leadership that moves stakeholders to think and work in new, initially unfamiliar ways. At the same time, principals also are called on to become less building managers and more instructional leaders (Fink & Resnick, 2001). These multiple levels of leadership must be coordinated, and leaders must align their efforts if successful change is to occur. In their research, Peter Youngs and M. Bruce King (2002) note that "Newmann, Smith, Allensworth, and Bryk (2001) found a strong relationship between program coherence and student achievement. . . ." (p. 646). Program coherence is more than management; it requires leadership.

Instructional leadership is a broad label, and some administrators have difficulty accepting and understanding the demands of instructional leadership—and fitting instructional leadership responsibilities into already crowded workloads. According to Schmoker (1999), principals' reluctance to take on instructional leadership can mean that, despite a school's official adoption of new programs, the reality behind the classroom door does not change. In such cases of superficial implementation, teachers find ways to twist the innovation back into what they have always done. This is not an indictment of teachers but a reflection of weak leadership that is incomplete and insufficient to produce and then support real change.

Various writers have identified four areas in which transparency is a marker of leadership:

- Clear purpose (Schmoker, 1999).
- Clear expectations (Marzano, 2003).

- Clear understanding (Williams, 1996).
- Clear feedback (Williams, 1996).

All four are interconnected and together provide a foundation for sustaining open and honest relationships with and among staff. Leaders need to have well-defined and articulated *purposes* or goals they wish to attain, both short- and long-term, which are clearly communicated to a staff (Schmoker, 1999). Leaders must make clear the behavioral *expectations* of their staff that are necessary to achieve this purpose (Marzano, 2003). Leaders need to be sure that staff *understand* what is expected as well as possess knowledge and skills necessary to perform the tasks (Williams, 1996). Finally, leaders need to use multiple methods to provide clear, concise *feedback* in order to assess progress, affirm direction, and support efforts to meet the established purpose (Williams, 1996).

At the forefront are principals. According to Zepeda (2004),

> Teachers will look to the principal for affirmation of their efforts at improvement. To this end, the principal needs to view school improvement as an opportunity to celebrate success, build relationships, appraise honestly where teachers and the school are, and forge a credible and meaningful plan for improvement. The school improvement process provides an opportunity for the principal to share power through openness, dialogue, and sincere desire to build trust. (pp. 14–15)

Not all leaders are transparent. There are two other degrees of clarity: translucent and opaque. *Translucent* can be defined as "admitting but diffusing light so that objects beyond cannot be clearly distinguished." Translucent leaders may be transparent in one or more of the four areas listed previously, but they will be vague in others. Such vagueness can cause confusion and diminish effectiveness. A small initial misunderstanding can turn have a "butterfly" effect so that over time it is magnified into a major problem. *Opaque* means "does not permit light to pass through." Opaque leaders make no attempt to either inform staff or include them in making decisions. Staff members are likely to be kept in the dark. Even if leaders have a clear sense of purpose, expectations, and feedback, if they fail to clearly understand and communicate, then they are opaque leaders.

UNDERSTANDING EVERYONE'S ROLE

Communication networks build trust through openness, or transparency. If individuals are free to talk with others, then personal agendas tend to disappear. If teachers have questions, they are free to ask whomever they want for an answer. Communication operates from teacher to teacher, teacher to coach, coach to principal, coach to central office staff, and all other combinations. But schools still operate in a hierarchy. There is a chain of command with individuals having assigned roles and responsibilities. Understanding these roles and the power that goes with them also is important for effective communication.

Coaches have the ability to influence actions in many ways, for example, by

- making expectations clear,
- sharing knowledge,
- sharing rationales,
- building rapport,
- providing verbal or written rewards or recognition,
- conducting positive one-on-one and small-group conversations,
- listening actively,
- modeling desired behaviors,
- supporting peer coaching,
- sharing power in making decisions,
- building collaborative energy, and
- providing follow-up training.

People often assume that when someone designated with "power" speaks, appropriate actions occur. But communication always gets translated through filters. Teachers' understandings and compliance will depend on how they perceive messages about change and their capacity to integrate new knowledge and skills with those they already possess. When things do not happen as coaches expect, it may be because teachers lack

- appropriate training,
- understanding of expectations,
- understanding of necessary behaviors, or
- understanding of differences between current and desired practices.

Teachers may be afraid to try innovations for a host of reasons, not least because they have received mixed messages from different sources.

Following is a scenario that illustrates how mathematics coaches can use the power of influence and persuasion:

Ms. Jones is a high school teacher with 10 years of experience. She is well respected by staff and liked by parents and students. She is willing to serve on committees and will volunteer her time freely.

Her students score well in her class and satisfactorily on state assessments. She is not in a formal leadership position. During classroom visits the mathematics coach has seen Ms. Jones allowing students to work on homework together in pairs or small groups, but her use of grouping is minimal and incomplete. The coach decides to discuss the issue in a one-on-one conversation.

Coach: As I have been doing classroom visits, I have noticed you allowing students to complete assignments in pairs or small groups. How is this working for you and the students?

Ms. Jones: The students really seem to enjoy this, and I am having more students completing their assignments.

Coach: Since the students enjoy working together, what other grouping strategies do you know or are using that I have not been in the class to see?

Ms. Jones: Well, I know some teachers are using grouping during instruction.

Coach: Have you tried grouping students during instruction?

Ms. Jones: I did once, but my students just didn't seem to want to work together.

Coach: As you said, your students do enjoy working on assignments together. Other teachers are finding that students also enjoy working together during instruction. What would help you include grouping strategies during a lesson?

Ms. Jones: I have some lessons next week that may work.

Coach: Great, can I help you set this up?

Ms. Jones: I think it will be okay.

Coach: I'm sure you will do great. When can I visit your room to see the grouping strategy in action? I know it can be challenging getting several groups going, so I would like to be there to help.

From this conversation the coach has gained a better understanding of Ms. Jones and should be able to assist her in incorporating additional and more effective grouping strategies. Ms. Jones has now heard that grouping strategies are important and that she should incorporate some strategies she knows but is not using. Moving forward, the coach may later suggest that Ms. Jones could benefit from working with another teacher, observing a classroom in which grouping is extensively used, planning a lesson with the coach, or coteaching with the coach.

Mathematics coaches should ensure that they use positive power. Negative power too often breaks trust and damages rapport. Following are three examples of statements the mathematics coach in the previous scenario might have said but wisely did not:

> "I want you to teach a lesson using grouping strategies, and I'll be there to observe."

> "I've talked to the principal, and he wants this strategy used."

> "You're the last teacher I would expect to be so difficult about using this strategy; everyone else is already on board."

Coaches are better served by positive influence, and teachers will respond accordingly.

Unfortunately, sometimes coaches get caught between principals and teachers. While a natural impulse is to provide immediate assistance to teachers, coaches often will find it more productive to take time to consider problems and solutions, rather than deciding something on the spur of the moment that will have to be rethought later. Here is an example:

> A middle school teacher catches the mathematics coach in the hall between classes. The teacher states that several students in his room are unable to multiply or divide fractions, and he is very frustrated. He does not feel he can help the students. He wants to move them out of his room to a remedial mathematics class.

This is a serious issue, but changing the students' class assignments is not a responsibility of the coach. Thus, the coach might respond with one of the following:

> "That's an important issue, and I know you need an answer. In this case, I think you need to ask your team leader or the principal. I would like to know what you find out. I will be glad to help you work with these students."

> "I don't know the answer to your request about moving the students, but I will try to find out and get back to you."

> "Thank you for your honesty. I need some time to think about this. I would like for you to think about it also. When can we get back together?"

Mathematics coaches must be part of many communication networks while maintaining a "balcony view" of the entire school. Transparency is vital to avoid pitfalls that can detract from improvement efforts.

SYNERGY: THE POWER OF GROUPS

Individuals have power and can exert influence. Working alone, individuals can accomplish much. But working with others increases positive outcomes. *Synergy* refers to the idea that the whole is greater than the sum of the parts. Cooperative interaction among individuals within a group and among various groups results in synergy.

We have illustrated that power can be negative or positive, and when positive power is exerted through transparency and influence, then positive outcomes can be achieved. Teachers exert positive power that complements mathematics coaches' efforts by

- studying new and unfamiliar instructional strategies and incorporating them into their classrooms,
- meeting with a partner after school to plan their mathematics lessons,
- sharing with each other their successes and concerns,
- working with colleagues to plan and evaluate assessments,
- working with partners to reflect on instructional practice,
- taking classes after school and during the summer to improve their knowledge and pedagogy, and
- participating in professional organizations.

Effective Group Behavior

Groups operate on a balance of formal and informal behaviors—behaviors that range from highly structured to spontaneous. Groups need sufficient structure to get things accomplished but sufficient informality to be enjoyable and allow for creativity. Garmston and Wellman (1999) identify four characteristics that individuals need to bring to working with a group:

1. To know one's intentions and choose congruent behaviors.

2. To set aside unproductive patterns of listening, responding, and inquiring.

3. To know when to self-assert and when to integrate.

4. To know and support the group's purposes, topics, processes, and development. (p. 34)

They further state, "Developing a staff's capabilities for talking together professionally is no panacea, but it may represent one of the single most significant investments that faculties can make for student learning" (p. 52). The message for mathematics coaches is that effective operating conditions, norms, or standards for groups will not simply emerge but must be developed.

When teachers work in groups, their actions are out in the open, so there can be communal learning. Teachers may begin to feel free to visit one another's classes and actively solve problems together. They focus on learning outcomes and their teaching as the means of achieving desired outcomes (Garmston & Wellman, 1999).

Effective group work requires a focused agenda with defined roles and responsibilities. Following are some topics on which teacher groups might focus to implement and sustain effective instructional improvement. The group might

- review mathematics content in curriculum documents, state standards, textbooks, and other materials for current, previous, and future lessons;
- review, analyze, and discuss student assessments;
- select and discuss appropriate instructional strategies;
- outline lesson processes, such as introduction, exploration, and summarization;
- reflect on the results of teaching a particular lesson;
- discuss and plan for effective interventions; and
- discuss and plan for addressing student misconceptions.

Professional Learning Communities

In working with groups, one goal of mathematics coaches should be to help form professional learning communities (PLCs). Isolation of teachers is a serious problem in many schools. Although the negative effects of isolation have been well documented, few school systems have effectively addressed this artifact of organizational structure. Isolation is the rule rather than the exception (Short & Greer, 2002). The professional learning community approach is based on the assumption that the purpose of education is to ensure not just that students are taught but that they learn (DuFour, 2004).

Collaborative efforts decrease teacher burnout and hence reduce teacher turnover (Inger, 1993). This result, in itself, is justification for structural changes. But true collaboration requires more than a shift in organization; it also requires a shift in philosophy. This higher purpose is more difficult to achieve, and it is the reason that many school systems, if they have attempted to change, have been unsuccessful in implementing necessary professional learning communities (Schmoker, 2004).

The struggle is worth the effort. There is a strong consensus that leadership and high-quality teaching are critical, if not the most critical, factors in school improvement. Classroom teachers' knowledge and skills are paramount in successful student learning, and instructional leadership is the most effective way of ensuring teacher quality (Reeves, 2006). Shared, collective thinking and learning are expedient ways to achieve school improvement. Collaboration brings an increased confidence level among staff.

Efficacy, the belief that one can make a difference, is a cornerstone of teacher instructional change (Huitt, 2000). The nature of collaboration is such that when it is used, more ideas and solutions are placed on the table for consideration. This increases the likelihood of effective lesson implementation, targets desired mathematics content, and increases content consistency and student access (Inger, 1993). Interaction among peers allows for support of individual strengths as well as support to overcome weaknesses. The structure also includes opportunities to close the learning gap between experienced and inexperienced teachers while providing a vehicle for inclusion and consideration of new and novel ideas (Schmoker, 2004).

The shift to true professional learning communities is a challenging one. According to Zepeda (2004), collaborative cultures have distinct characteristics:

- *Critical Elements.* Reflective dialogue, deprivatization of practice, collective focus on student learning, collaboration, and shared norms and values.
- *Structural Condition.* Time to meet and talk, physical proximity, inter-dependent teaching roles, communications structures, and teacher empowerment.
- *Social and Human Factors.* Openness to improvement, trust and respect, cognitive and skill-based teaching and learning, supportive leadership, and socialization of teachers. (p. 43)

In summary, when collaboratively planning lessons or instructional units, teachers discuss mathematics content, instructional strategies, materials, prior student learning, and common assessments. By providing time and support for planning common lessons or instructional units, leaders—mathematics coaches, principals, curriculum directors—greatly increase the likelihood that an adopted instructional program will be implemented to a high degree of reliability and fidelity. In turn, this higher degree of implementation increases the likelihood that students, regardless of their classroom assignment, will learn the necessary content.

CRITICAL POINTS

Mathematics coaches operate within an education system. Although the system occasionally creates roadblocks, it also provides coaches with the power and influence needed to accomplish their objectives. Individual power is multiplied as coaches exert leadership rather than management, work toward transparency, and structure and participate in groups with the aim that some groups, over time, will become fully functioning professional learning communities.

11 Sustaining Momentum

Mathematics coaches—current and prospective—who have worked their way through this book have examined philosophies, concepts, and strategies targeted to improve teaching and learning. Among other things, we have suggested that it is vital for coaches to be a presence in classrooms and to work directly with teachers as much as possible, whether that happens one on one or in groups.

Classroom teachers ultimately make the difference in student learning. Daily intersections of content, activities, materials, and students are significant. When mathematics coaches collaboratively plan and coteach lessons, they gain valuable knowledge about what teachers know and can do in actual instructional interactions. This knowledge permits coaches to tailor their efforts in ways that are beneficial for effective change.

Teachers—and others, including principals and parents—may resist change for any number of reasons. They may be uncomfortable with change generally or with a specific change they are being asked to make. They may not see the benefit of change. And teachers, in particular, may feel as though they, not mathematics coaches, are in the best position to judge what students need to learn and how best to teach them.

Throughout this book we have attempted to provide strategies in a sequential framework to help mathematics coaches overcome resistance and reluctance. In the end the key to success will come down to planned, thoughtful persistence. Coaches must start small in many cases and then build new initiatives on the success of earlier ones. Tackling a manageable number of initiatives is more productive than taking a scattershot approach.

MANAGING LONG-TERM CHANGE

Achieving long-term change takes time and persistence, often in the face of serious opposition. Expending the mental and physical energy to reach significant goals in improving teaching and learning can be wearing. Mathematics coaches often will feel as though the stress and pressures will never end, and progress will never come. They may feel thwarted in every attempt aimed at trying something new or different.

Mathematics coaches may sense futility and frustration, but they must be confident that persistence will pay off. Setbacks are normal. And strategies that work with some teachers do not work with others. The majority of teachers will change their instructional strategies under the right conditions and with the right leadership. The influence to change frequently is a result of peer communication and peer pressure from working in groups. Just as students become active learners when they are allowed and encouraged to direct their own learning, so too will teachers become engaged in change and improvement when they gain ownership of the change process. Coaches are instrumental in getting this to happen.

Self-motivated teachers will continually work at improving their performance. They will constantly perfect their abilities to design and present lessons. They will continually update and expand their repertoires of instructional strategies. These are teachers who will read about teaching, discuss teaching, and gladly, eagerly attend professional training sessions about teaching. Coaches who work with highly motivated teachers need to help these teachers focus their energies and ensure that they take on only a reasonable, manageable number of strategies at one time. There is a hazard if too many strategies are attempted. Failure can result because too many variables are introduced in a lesson and so many things happen that analysis and reflection may not be able to pinpoint strengths or weaknesses.

In managing long-term change effective mathematics coaches understand that innovations move through initiating, implementing, and then institutionalizing phases (Kaser et al., 2002). While change is occurring, teachers' abilities to use innovations also move through phases: novice, master, and then expert. Successful coaches must be mindful of these phases and work to ensure that teachers do not plateau at the novice phase, which often happens when change is mandated rather than developed and supported.

USING C-BAM

One well-documented change model is the Concerns-Based Adoption Model (C-BAM) from Hall and Hord (2001), which points out that adults move through predictable processing stages when they are faced with change.

In adopting an innovation, they follow the stages shown in Figure 11.1, beginning at the bottom and moving to the top.

Figure 11.1	Stages of Concern About the Innovation
6	Refocusing: exploration of more universal beliefs
5	Collaboration: coordination and cooperation
4	Consequence: impact of the innovation on students
3	Management: processes and tasks related to the innovation
2	Personal: uncertainty of demands
1	Informational: general awareness
0	Awareness: little or no concern

SOURCE: Hall & Hord, 2001, p. 63.

Mathematics coaches who are aware of this model can carefully listen to teachers and then make appropriate decisions that both support teachers' concerns and help move them to the next level. When coaches are involved in coplanning lessons, group work, and reflective processes, they have multiple opportunities to hear teachers' concerns and identify the levels at which teachers are operating.

There is no set time for each stage of C-BAM, because people change or adapt at different rates, but the stages themselves are fairly well established. For example, teachers working at the management stage (Level 3) are focused on how an innovation works in their classrooms, based on their current knowledge. They are not ready to look at the actual consequences of an innovation. When helping these teachers reflect on their lessons and incorporate a new strategy, mathematics coaches will find this insight helpful.

Another important aspect of the change process is diffusion. According to Rogers (1995), diffusion refers to how an innovation or strategy filters through a system or network and is adopted by its members. Diffusion is a social process of adopting a new behavior that is affected by peers. In Rogers's view, diffusion may lead teachers to use a new strategy even if scientific evidence suggests that the strategy is not effective. Several critical factors are involved in diffusion that are important for mathematics coaches to know. Rogers notes five:

1. **Relative Advantage.** Is it better than the current idea?

2. **Compatibility.** Is it consistent with current values, experiences, and needs?

3. **Complexity.** Is it easy or difficult to understand and use?

4. **Trialability.** Can it be partially implemented and experimented with?

5. **Observability.** Are there visible results? (p. 206)

While identifying each innovation or strategy according to these five characteristics may be difficult for mathematics coaches, ignoring them would be unwise. This is particularly true for the second and third characteristics, compatibility and complexity, because teachers often are asked to implement strategies that do not align with their current instructional practices and, perhaps more important, do not fit into their current approach to lesson flow and design.

Adoption and diffusion stages play an important role in determining why some new strategies are readily employed and others are not. Personality characteristics and tendencies also influence the pace of adoption. These characteristics are not rigid categories, but most people generally favor one end of a continuum that, according to Rogers (1995), includes the following descriptors, in order: innovators, early adopters, early majority, late majority, and laggards (p. 255). The categories are self-explanatory. While mathematics coaches may want to substitute a less negative term for "laggards," the sense is clear. These are teachers who are reluctant or unwilling to adopt new instructional strategies.

Regardless of labels, teachers will adapt to change and embrace new ideas and strategies at varying rates. According to Rogers,

> The greatest response to change agent efforts occurs when opinion leaders adopt, which usually occurs somewhere between 3 and 16 percent adoption in most systems. The innovation will then continue to spread with little promotion by change agents, after a critical mass of adopters is reached. (p. 208)

Additionally, Rogers notes, opinion leaders usually are early adopters, but not innovators. Mathematics coaches need to be aware that a few vocal, enthusiastic teachers embracing change may mask a "silent majority" who are not. Mathematics coaches need to assess the pace of change and the extent of diffusion to be sure that improvement is occurring throughout the network or system.

TIPPING POINTS AND BREAKTHROUGHS

Schmoker (2004), borrowing the idea from Malcolm Gladwell (2002), writes about a "tipping point" of innovation. The idea is somewhat like a balance scale that has an unknown amount of weight on one end.

Mathematics coaches, through their efforts with individuals and groups, continually add weight to the other side. The scale gradually moves and then suddenly tips to the weightier side—the side of change. A tipping point is impossible to predict; it just happens.

According to Schmoker, the tipping point is when change reaches a critical mass of adoption. By this, he means that "we have to reach a 'tipping point,' the moment when—sometimes quite quickly—peoples' actions and attitudes change dramatically, and the change spreads like a contagion. Such change typically happens through an energized word-of-mouth campaign" (p. 431). The message for mathematics coaches is that persistence in providing data, introducing new strategies, and offering ongoing support will, at some point, result in change becoming not an individual or a small-group phenomenon but a systemic one. Change will reach the tipping point and become institutionalized.

The idea of a tipping point is reinforced by Collins (2001) in his book, *Good to Great*. Collins draws on an image of a flywheel, with change as the energy needed to spin it. A leader (in our case, a mathematics coach) pushes and pushes, and the wheel slowly rotates. Then at an unexplained and undefined time, the flywheel uses its own weight to assist in spinning—the breakthrough point (pp. 164–165). Mathematics coaches can envision what such a flywheel of change looks like in motion and what it can accomplish. This vision is important, but Collins adds another important quality: a climate of truth. Leadership engenders a climate of truth that helps mathematics coaches know where they are and encourages them to keep pushing toward the breakthrough, the tipping point, when change is propelled by its own momentum.

According to Collins, creating this climate of truth embodies four themes. These themes apply to coaching in this way:

First, mathematics coaches lead with questions, not answers.

Second, mathematics coaches encourage dialogue and debate without coercion.

Third, mathematics coaches dissect the facts without looking to place blame.

Fourth, mathematics coaches establish agreed-on signals for raising issues and concerns in a timely manner.

The three main writers whom we have cited in this chapter—Rogers, Schmoker, and Collins—all focus on a pivot point of change. Undergirding this point, however, is their emphasis on communication networks that, in effect, set the flywheel spinning and build the momentum that results in the tipping point effect. Another point these authors make is that persistence pays off. In order to achieve implementation, mathematics coaches have to persist in their efforts.

STAYING FOCUSED ON WHAT MATTERS

Leadership from mathematics coaches is needed not only to set a climate and provide initial and subsequent pushes on the flywheel but also to choose a correct flywheel. There is a tendency in education to have far too many flywheels, all being pushed at the same time.

Educators—whether mathematics coaches, teachers, principals, or others—do not have sufficient time or energy to be pushing the wrong flywheel or too many flywheels. If coaches want to achieve true and lasting change, then they must decide where to focus their attention. Failure to do so will undermine not only any current change initiative but future innovations as well. Throughout this book we have provided focal points; three can be summarized as follows:

Curriculum. Aligning content, standards, strategies, materials, and assessments is a vital focus for any effort to improve teaching and learning. Among the most important strategic shifts in instruction is one that moves teachers from being presenters of content to facilitators of learning. Students become active learners, supported by classroom environments of collaboration that mix teacher–student and student–student interactions with individual initiative.

Data Gathering and Analysis. Data support and propel change initiatives. Teachers need to see that their efforts are working. This means data collection must be timely, and accurate data must be collected. Teachers must be able to trust that data will be used to inform practice, not to evaluate, critique, or reprimand. Data also are used to study trends over time.

Collaboration. Teachers share ideas, knowledge, and expertise. When mathematics coaches and teachers work together, for example, in collaborative planning or coteaching, they create change that is sustainable. When teachers work in networks, they can transform education systems.

THE POWER OF ONE

It is fitting to end this book with a story. Everyone knows stories of a charismatic leader who emerges to take charge of a serious situation and save the day. These leaders range from fictional superheroes to real, down-to-earth, everyday heroes—like the folks who show up every day and work, as mathematics coaches and teachers do, to improve their corners of the world.

Trying to achieve true school reform can seem overwhelming. But mathematics coaches can and do accomplish sustainable improvement in teaching and learning. Dweck (2006) relates the story of Thomas Edison. Most people know from history books that Edison is credited with creating—inventing or at least perfecting—the light bulb. The point that sometimes is missed is that Edison was not a solo super-scientist. He did not work in isolation. He had a laboratory full of highly intelligent, creative scientists who collaborated in the endeavor to achieve a working light bulb.

But we also must remember that it was Edison who gathered these scientists into teams. He pulled them together and helped them focus their time and energy on solving a particularly important problem. He encouraged them to learn from each other and to build on shared knowledge. Thus, they shared their successes and learned from their failures.

In a very real sense, Edison did not invent the light bulb; collaboration did. Yet it was Edison's influence and his ability to build networks that resulted in such a tremendous scientific advance. The power of one individual is magnified by those with whom that individual works. Mathematics coaches have the power of one.

Resource A

Statistical Definitions

Definitions

closed response: A test question with only one correct answer.

common assessment: A test item administered at an established time to every student in the same course or grade.

criterion-referenced test: An assessment designed to reveal what a student knows, understands, or can do in relation to specific objectives. Criterion-referenced tests are intended to identify strengths and weaknesses in individual students in terms of knowledge or skills.

free response: A task with multiple paths to explore and multiple solutions to the answer.

multiple choice: A test item with a controlled number of responses from which the student must select an answer.

norm-referenced test: A standardized assessment designed to place a student or group of students in rank order compared to other test takers of the same age and grade.

open-ended response: A performance task in which students are given a stimulus or prompt and then asked to communicate a response. Tasks may be more or less open depending on how many restrictions or directions are included.

reliability: A measure of the constancy of scoring outcomes over time or over many evaluators. A test is considered reliable if the same answers produce the same score no matter when and how the scoring is done.

rubric: An established set of criteria for scoring or rating students' tests, portfolios, or performances.

validity: A measure of how well an assessment relates to what students are expected to have learned. A valid assessment measures what it is supposed to measure and not some peripheral features.

Definitions from:

Hart, D. (1994). *Authentic assessment: A handbook for educators.* Menlo Park, CA: Addison-Wesley, pp. 105–114.

Resource B

Mapping Principles and Classroom Vision

A Reflective Guide

Coaches, in order to move forward, are to occasionally look back. At the beginning of this book, two big ideas were presented—the National Council of Teachers of Mathematics (NCTM) and National Council of Supervisors of Mathematics (NCSM) principles and the vision of the futuristic, high-quality mathematics program as depicted in an effective mathematics classroom. Obviously, these two ideas are highly correlated. Achieving the principles also achieves the vision of the desired classroom. It is now time for mathematics coaches to reflect upon their progress, take stock of successes and misses, establish a new baseline, and prepare to repeat the entire process outlined in this book.

The job, of course, never ends. There are always things to learn or techniques to perfect. The reflective process is based on actual experience of the coaches, data gathered through various sources, and the professional opinion of the coaches and, perhaps, some of their colleagues.

The reflective process, at this point, is intended to focus on the NCTM and NCSM principles of

- equity,
- curriculum,
- teaching,
- learning, and
- assessment.

These principles are combined with the traits of a desired high-quality mathematics program found in Chapter 3, "Bridging the Present and Future." These traits are

1. teachers are empowered,

2. curriculum is implemented as designed,

3. multiple instructional strategies are employed,

4. students are actively engaged, and

5. assessment is varied.

Matching the principles to the traits provides the following pairings:

Equity is directly related to the empowering of teachers,

curriculum is directly related to implementing the curriculum as designed,

teaching is directly related to employing multiple instructional strategies,

learning is directly related to actively engaging the students, and

assessment is directly related to using a variety of assessment methods.

Equity Related to Teacher Empowerment

The equity principle is in place when all students are provided the opportunity to learn the appropriate mathematics curriculum. This opportunity is directly related to the content, but it also is related to inclusive instructional techniques that bring students into the learning process. The empowerment of teachers is related to efficacy—the belief that all students can learn meaningful mathematics and the teacher has the ability to actually teach it to the students.

Evidence: This "can-do" attitude of empowered teachers is demonstrated by their willingness to do whatever it takes for students to stay engaged and to learn. Coaches will no longer hear such statements as "they can't," or "they won't." They will hear statements such as "That didn't seem to work too well," "What else can I try?" and "What did you do?"

Curriculum Related to Implementation

The curriculum principle is in place when every teacher is teaching the mathematics content identified by a district and directly aligned to state-mandated standards.

Evidence: Mathematics coaches will routinely see teachers referencing their curriculum documents while planning. Teachers will be highly conversant with state standards and the organization of district documents.

Teaching Related to Multiple Strategies

The teaching principle is in place when teachers are meaningfully using a variety of instructional strategies. Furthermore, the strategies are intentionally selected based upon the content to be taught, the misconceptions students tend to have, and how the strategies help make student thinking visible and overt.

Evidence: The strategies are included in lesson plans, shared with other teachers, and routinely discussed as to the degree of effectiveness. Strategies are constantly being revised and refined. Mathematics coaches will see evidence of this in coplanning and coteaching sessions. Coaches will hear the conversations at a rich level of analysis during group meetings.

Learning Related to Student Engagement

The learning principle is in place when students are active participants in the classroom. Students are talking and discussing, gathering and analyzing data, making predictions, and justifying their thinking.

Evidence: Teachers are still leading the classroom, but not necessarily from the front of the room, and certainly not by monopolizing the conversation. Coaches will see evidence of this while coteaching. They will also hear evidence during planning sessions and group meetings.

Assessment Related to Variety

The assessment principle is in place when teachers select and use a variety of ways in which to determine the degree of student learning. Teachers recognize that students need to demonstrate what they know in order to make the knowledge clearer to the students themselves and clearer to the teacher.

Evidence: Students routinely show their work and explain their thinking. Formative and summative assessments are in constant use. More importantly, teachers actually used the collected data to inform their instructional practices. When they discuss teaching and teaching strategies, they have evidence of which practices worked and which did not in the given situations. Coaches will see evidence of the data and progress of learning. They will also be involved in helping teachers reflect upon their practices.

Teacher Beliefs

Although more difficult perhaps to identify, mathematics coaches are also to seek evidence of changing teacher beliefs. These beliefs, again from Chapter 3, are as follows:

All students can learn mathematics.

Teachers can teach students.

Mathematics is conceptual and developmental.

These beliefs are intertwined with the principles and with the initial principle of equity. As beliefs change, coaches will hear a change in how teachers talk about the students and the mathematics.

Evidence: Teachers will take much more ownership and responsibility for learning. Learning mathematics will no longer be attributed to the "math gene" or "good parenting" but rather to classroom instruction the students were given.

THE CYCLIC NATURE

The cycle repeats. Prepared with the above information, mathematics coaches establish a new baseline. Teachers, coaches, principals, schools, and the students have moved from point A to point B on the continuum improvement scale.

Coaches are to be honest but not overly self-critical. There are many factors to be considered. The educational system is still operating.

Resource C

Transparent Communication + Positive Power Actions + Domains of Power:

Power of Position—granted by district, chain of command

Analyzing current conditions—have you been up front with the staff?

Making clear expectations—have you actually told the staff what you want done?

Sharing power—have you included staff in the decision process?

Modeling—have you used the desired behaviors or techniques?

Power of Knowledge/Expertise—achievements, experience

Sharing knowledge—have you provided the staff with the data?

Sharing rationale—have you explained your reasoning and the basis for your decision, concern, or need?

Providing follow-up training—is it needed by group or individual?

Power of Reward/Recognition—tacit or overt

Verbal—have you specifically recognized individual staff efforts? (overt)

　　　—have you specifically recognized group efforts? (tacit)

Written—have you specifically recognized individual staff efforts? (overt)

　　　—have you specifically recognized group efforts? (tacit)

Power of Persuasion—communication, solicit support

Conducting one-on-one—have you talked to the individual alone?

Conducting small group—have you talked with small groups of staff?

Power of Peers—using leaders, critical mass

Supporting peer coaching—have you used leaders to bring on or support staff?

Building collaborative energy—have you asked small groups to offer recommendations?

Resource D

Leadership Styles That Get Results by Daniel Goleman from The Institute for Management Excellence, located at http://www.itstime.com/mar2003.htm.

Coercive Leadership Style: "Do what I tell you."

- Demands immediate compliance.
- May be used in a crisis to address a problem or a difficult employee.
- Has a **negative** impact on the climate.
- Power of coercion.

Pacesetting Leadership Style: "Do as I do, now."

- Sets a high standard of performance.
- Used to get quick results from a highly motivated and competent team.
- Has a **negative** impact on the climate.
- Power of position.

Affiliative Leadership Style: "People come first."

- Creates harmony and builds emotional bonds.
- Used to heal rifts in a team or to motivate people during stressful circumstances.
- Has a **positive** impact on the climate.
- Power of reward/recognition.

Democratic Leadership Style: "What do you think?"

- Forges consensus through participation.
- Used to build buy-in or consensus or to get input from valuable employees.

- Has a **positive** impact on the climate.
- Power of peers.

Coaching Leadership Style: "Try this."

- Develops people for the future.
- Used to help employee improve performance or develop long-term strengths.
- Has a **positive** impact on the climate.
- Power of knowledge/expertise.

Authoritative Leadership Style: "Come with me."

- Mobilizes people toward a vision.
- Used when changes require a new vision or a clear direction.
- Has a strongly **positive** impact on the climate.
- Power of persuasion.

References

Achieve. (2006). *Closing the expectations gap: An annual 50-state progress report on the alignment of high school policies with the demands of college and work.* Washington, DC: Author

Adelman, C. (2006). *The toolbox revisited: Paths to degree completion from high school through college.* Washington DC: U.S. Department of Education.

Boaler, J. (2006). Urban success: A multidimensional mathematics approach with equitable outcomes. *Phi Delta Kappan, 87*(5), 364–369.

Caine, R., & Caine, G. (1994). *Making connections: Teaching and the human brain.* Menlo Park, CA: Addison-Wesley.

Coleman, J. S. et al. (1966). *Equality of educational opportunity.* Washington, DC: U.S. Department of Health, Education, and Welfare, Office of Education.

Collins, J. (2001). *Good to great.* New York: Harper Collins.

Conzemius, A., & O'Neill, J. (2001). *Building shared responsibility for student learning.* Alexandria, VA: Association for Supervision and Curriculum Development.

Covey, S. (1991). *Principle-centered leadership.* New York: Summit Books.

Cushman, K. (2003). *Fires in the bathroom: Advice for teachers from high school students.* New York: The New Press.

DuFour, R. (2004). The best staff development is in the workplace, not in a workshop. *Journal of Staff Development, 25*(2), 63–64.

Dweck, C. (2006). *Mindset: The new psychology of success.* New York: Random House.

English, F. (2000). *Deciding what to teach and test.* Thousand Oaks, CA: Corwin.

Felux, C., & Snowdy, P. (Eds.). (2006). *The math coach field guide: Charting your course.* Sausalito, CA: Math Solutions.

Fink, E., & Resnick, L. (2001). Developing principals as instructional leaders. *Phi Delta Kappan, 81*(4), 598–606.

Fullan, M. (1993). *Change forces.* London, UK: The Falmer Press.

Garmston, R., & Wellman, B. (1999). *The adaptive school: A sourcebook for developing groups.* Norwood, MA: Christopher-Gordon.

Gladwell, M. (2002). *The tipping point: How little things can make a big difference.* Boston: Little, Brown.

Hall, G., & Hord, S. (2001). *Implementing change: Patterns, principles, and potholes.* Needham Heights, MA: Allyn & Bacon.

Huitt, W. (2000). *Teacher efficacy.* Educational Psychology Interactive. Valdosta, GA: Valdosta State University. Retrieved February 23, 2009, from http://chiron.valdosta.edu/whuitt/col/teacher/tcheff.html

Inger, M. (1993). *Teacher collaboration in secondary schools* (Centerfocus Number 2). Berkeley: National Center for Research in Vocational Education, University of California.

Institute for Management Excellence. (2008). *Leadership styles that get results.* Retrieved August 19, 2008, from http://www.itstime.com/mar2003.htm

Jensen, E. (1998). *Teaching with the brain in mind.* Alexandria, VA: Association for Supervision and Curriculum Development.

Kaser, J., Mundry, S., Stiles, K., & Loucks-Horsley, S. (2002). *Leading every day: 124 actions for effective leadership.* Thousand Oaks, CA: Corwin.

Kennedy, M. (2005). *Inside teaching: How classroom life undermines reform.* Cambridge, MA: Harvard University Press.

Knight, J. (2007). *Instructional coaching: A partnership approach to improving instruction.* Thousand Oaks, CA: Corwin.

Lewin's leadership styles. (n.d.). Retrieved August 19, 2008, from http://changingminds .org/disciplines/leadership/styles/lewin_style.htm

Loucks-Horsley, S., Love, N., Stiles, K., Mundry, S., & Hewson, P. (2003). *Designing professional development for teachers of science and mathematics.* Thousand Oaks, CA: Corwin.

Love, N. (2002). *Using data/getting results: A practical guide for school improvement in mathematics and science.* Norwood, MA: Christopher-Gordon.

Marzano, R. (2003). *What works in schools: Translating research into action.* Alexandria, VA: Association for Supervision and Curriculum Development.

Marzano, R., Pickering, D., & Pollock, J. (2001). *Classroom instruction that works: Research-based strategies for increasing student achievement.* Alexandria, VA: Association for supervision and Curriculum Development.

National Center for Education Statistics. (various years). *Trends in International Mathematics and Science Study (TIMSS).* Washington, DC: U.S. Department of Education. Available at http://nces.ed.gov/timss

National Commission on Mathematics and Science Teaching for the 21st Century. (2000). *Before it's too late: A report to the nation from the national commission on mathematics and science teaching for the 21st century.* Washington, DC: U.S. Department of Education.

National Council of Supervisors of Mathematics. (2008). *The PRIME leadership framework: Principles and indicators for mathematics leaders.* Bloomington, IN: Solution Tree.

National Council of Teachers of Mathematics. (2000). *Principles and standards for school mathematics.* Reston, VA: Author.

National Council of Teachers of Mathematics. (2006). *Curriculum focal points.* Reston, VA: Author.

National Mathematics Advisory Panel. (2008). *Foundations for success: The final report of the National Mathematics Advisory Panel.* Washington, DC: U.S. Department of Education.

National Research Council. (1999). *Improving student learning: A strategic plan for education research and its utilization.* Washington, DC: National Academy Press.

National Research Council. (2000). *How people learn: Brain, mind, experience, and school.* Washington, DC: National Academy Press.

National Research Council. (2001). *Adding it up: Helping children learn mathematics.* Washington, DC: National Academy Press.

National Research Council. (2002). *Helping children learn mathematics.* Washington DC: National Academy Press.

National Research Council. (2004a). *Engaging schools: Fostering high school students' motivation to learn.* Washington, DC: National Academy Press.

National Research Council. (2004b). *On evaluating curricular effectiveness: Judging the quality of K–12 mathematics evaluations.* Washington, DC: National Academy Press.

National Research Council. (2005). *How students learn: History, mathematics, and science in the classroom.* Washington, DC: National Academy Press.

Reeves, D. (2004). *Accountability for learning: How teachers and school leaders can take charge.* Alexandria, VA: Association for Supervision and Curriculum Development.

Reeves, D. (2006). *The learning leader: How to focus school improvement for better results.* Alexandria, VA: Association for Supervision and Curriculum Development.

Reys, R., Lindquist, M., Lambdin, D., Smith, N., & Suydam, M. (2007). *Helping children learn mathematics.* New York: John Wiley & Sons.

Rogers, E. (1995). *Diffusion of innovations.* New York: The Free Press.

Schmoker, M. (1999). *Results: The key to continuous school improvement.* Alexandria, VA: Association for Supervision and Curriculum Development.

Schmoker, M. (2004). Tipping point: From feckless reform to substantive instructional improvement. *Phi Delta Kappan, 85*(5), 424–432.

Senge, P., Cambron-McCabe, N., Lucas, T., Smith, B., Dutton, J., & Kleiner, A. (2000). *Schools that learn: A fifth discipline fieldbook for educators, parents, and everyone who cares about education.* New York: Doubleday.

Short, P. M., & Greer, J. T. (2002). *Leadership in empowered schools: Themes from innovative efforts.* Columbus, OH: Merrill Prentice Hall.

Spillane, J., Diamond, J., Burch, P., Hallett, T., Jita, L., & Zoltners, J. (2002). Managing in the middle: School leaders and the enactment of accountability policy. *Educational Policy, 16*(5), 731–762.

Starnes, B. A. (2006). What we don't know can hurt them: White teachers, Indian children. *Phi Delta Kappan, 87*(5), 364–369.

Stronge, J. (2007). *Qualities of effective teachers.* Alexandria, VA: Association for Supervision and Curriculum Development.

Ten types of power. (n.d.). Retrieved February 23, 2009, from http://www.everyonenegotiates.com/negotiation/tentypesofpower.htm

Thompson, S. (2003). Creating a high-performance school system. *Phi Delta Kappan, 84*(7), 489–495.

Tye, K. A., & Tye, B. B. (1984). Teacher isolation and school reform. *Phi Delta Kappan, 65*(5), 319–322.

Wagner, S. (Ed.). (2005). *PRompt intervention in mathematics education.* Columbus: Ohio Resource Center for Mathematics, Science, and Reading.

West, L., & Staub, F. (2003). *Content-focused coaching: Transforming mathematics lessons.* Portsmouth, NH: Heinemann.

Williams, B. (1996). *Closing the achievement gap: A vision for changing beliefs and practices.* Alexandria, VA: Association for Supervision and Curriculum Development.

York-Barr, J., Sommers, W., Ghere, G., & Montie, J. (2001). *Reflective practice to improve schools: An action guide for educators.* Thousand Oaks, CA: Corwin.

Youngs, P., & King, M. (2002). Principal leadership for professional development to build school capacity. *Educational Administration Quarterly, 38*(5), 643–670.

Zepeda, S. (2004). *Instructional leadership for school improvement.* Larchmont, NY: Eye on Education.

Index

CORWIN

A SAGE Company

The Corwin logo—a raven striding across an open book—represents the union of courage and learning. Corwin is committed to improving education for all learners by publishing books and other professional development resources for those serving the field of PreK–12 education. By providing practical, hands-on materials, Corwin continues to carry out the promise of its motto: **"Helping Educators Do Their Work Better."**